Martin Kramer
EDITOR-IN-CHIEF

Best Practices in Higher Education Consortia: How Institutions Can Work Together

Lawrence G. Dotolo
Virginia Tidewater Consortium for Higher Education

Jean T. Strandness
Tri-College University

EDITORS

Number 106, Summer 1999

JOSSEY-BASS PUBLISHERS
San Francisco

BEST PRACTICES IN HIGHER EDUCATION CONSORTIA: HOW INSTITUTIONS
CAN WORK TOGETHER
Lawrence G. Dotolo, Jean T. Strandness (eds.)
New Directions for Higher Education, no. 106
Volume XXVII, Number 2
Martin Kramer, Editor-in-Chief

Microfilm copies of issues and articles are available in 16mm and 35mm,
as well as microfiche in 105mm, through University Microfilms Inc., 300
North Zeeb Road, Ann Arbor, Michigan 48106–1346.

ISSN 0271-0560   ISBN 0-7879-4858-6

NEW DIRECTIONS FOR HIGHER EDUCATION is part of The Jossey-Bass
Higher and Adult Education Series and is published quarterly by Jossey-
Bass Inc., Publishers, 350 Sansome Street, San Francisco, California
94104–1342. Periodicals postage paid at San Francisco, California, and at
additional mailing offices. Postmaster: Send address changes to New
Directions for Student Services, Jossey-Bass Inc., Publishers, 350 Sansome
Street, San Francisco, California 94104–1342.

SUBSCRIPTIONS cost $56.00 for individuals and $99.00 for institutions,
agencies, and libraries. See Ordering Information page at end of book.

EDITORIAL CORRESPONDENCE should be sent to the Editor-in-Chief,
Martin Kramer, 2807 Shasta Road, Berkeley, California 94104-1342.

Cover photograph and random dot by Richard Blair/Color & Light
© 1990.

Jossey-Bass Web address: www.josseybass.com

in the United States of America on acid-free recycled paper con-
percent recovered waste paper, of which at least 20 percent is
r waste.

CONTENTS

EDITORS' NOTES

While college costs have spiraled upward over the last decade, so have complaints about higher education and demands that educational institutions be accountable to an increasing number of constituencies. As they have looked for ways to save money and to become more efficient while sustaining program quality, colleges and universities have shown increasing interest in consortial enterprises.

Realizing that the most current information about consortial cooperation among institutions needed to be made available to the educational community, the Association for Consortium Leadership, the national organization for consortia in the United States, decided to solicit from its members examples of what institutions of higher education working together can do. The contributors to this volume are all accomplished executive officers of consortia. Drawing on their direct knowledge and in some instances providing case studies, they offer practical advice, distilled from years of experience, on a variety of matters. They give specific examples of the activities in which consortia around the country are involved, with the view that others may learn from these models. The accounts of cooperative ventures contained in this volume should prove invaluable both to institutions of higher education currently involved in consortial enterprises and to those contemplating forming such alliances.

The subjects of the chapters in this book were selected for their potential interest to the greatest number of educators. They represent activities and programs that existing consortia have already attempted and refined, and they can be replicated or modified by other institutions of higher education to suit their needs. The chapters can be read in any order, and each can stand alone, so readers can select topics that are particularly germane to their own situation.

Colleges and universities can benefit in many ways from sharing resources. This sharing can involve library cooperation, cross-registration, the use of technology, and the joint purchasing of goods and services. It can include collaborative admissions and recruitment, faculty development, joint academic majors, international programs, economic development, and fundraising. These programs and services are discussed at length in this volume and should provide the reader with a basic understanding of how such forms of cooperation are accomplished. The volume also offers chapters on the process of starting a consortium and the role of consortium directors. In addition, an annotated bibliography provides readers with further references about consortia and collaborative practices.

The Association for Consortium Leadership sponsors conferences on cooperative ventures among institutions of higher education, publishes a newsletter for its members, and maintains a professional listserve. The association, which can be reached through its web page [www.acl.odu.edu], will

NEW DIRECTIONS FOR HIGHER EDUCATION, no. 106, Summer 1999 © Jossey-Bass Publishers

assist institutions of higher education in their efforts to form cooperative agreements and partnerships. The association also maintains a list of experienced consortium directors willing to serve as consultants.

Working on this volume has been an important collegial enterprise, and the editors would like to thank all the authors for their excellent contributions and helpful suggestions. Finally, we are grateful to Helen Johnson, staff member of the Virginia Tidewater Consortium, for her assistance in the preparation of this volume and to Nicola Beltz, assistant to the president and secretary to the board of directors of the Association for Consortium Leadership, for her invaluable help in keeping the project organized and on task.

Lawrence G. Dotolo
Jean T. Strandness
Editors

LAWRENCE G. DOTOLO is president of the Virginia Tidewater Consortium for Higher *tion and serves as executive director of the Association for Consortium Lead- *ith offices at Old Dominion University, Norfolk, Virginia.

*DNESS is provost of the Tri-College University consortium in Moorhead, *argo, North Dakota.

Starting an academic consortium is a relatively straightforward process, but ensuring its survival and effectiveness is a complex endeavor.

Starting and Sustaining a Consortium

Frederick Baus, Claire A. Ramsbottom

Over the past forty years colleges and universities have come together to form academic consortia for a variety of reasons. The initial wave of the formation of higher education consortia occurred in the 1960s and 1970s. Colleges entered into agreements to address common issues through cooperative initiatives in response to student needs, economic pressures, and federal government incentives. The institutions that form Five Colleges, Inc., in western Massachusetts, for example, originally came together in response to the large number of veterans taking advantage of the opportunities for higher education that became available to them after World War II. Later, the U.S. Department of Education provided significant financial incentives for consortia formed on the basis of shared faculty development programming. Student unrest, especially in the late 1960s and early 1970s, and difficult economic times also thrust college leaders together to commiserate and to discuss the value of interinstitutional cooperation. Unfortunately, many consortia formed during this wave of cooperation have not survived the loss of external motivation and external support.

The current wave of consortium formation, a phenomenon of the 1990s, also responds to a variety of conditions and incentives. The rise of information and communication technologies has increased pressures on institutions not only to be more competitive but to be more efficient. A growing understanding that organizations are not totally independent but are, in fact, interdependent and that strategic institutional management frequently entails partnerships has begun to have an impact on higher education. Board and community leadership expect that institutions will work together rather than compete unnecessarily and inefficiently. Further, the rising consumer cost of higher education (costs are rising faster than the rate of inflation) has led to national studies of the causes and cures for the rise, among which is the use of collaborative strategies to help control costs.

New Directions for Higher Education, no. 106, Summer 1999 © Jossey-Bass Publishers

How can we be assured that academic consortia created under this second wave of collaborative enthusiasm will fare better and survive longer than those created during the first wave? This chapter will offer insights that focus expectations and demystify academic consortia, aiding their success and survival.

Definition of Consortium

What exactly is an academic consortium? In the early 1970s, Lewis Patterson, working out of the Kansas City Regional Council for Higher Education, created a national network of academic consortia—initially the Council for Inter-Institutional Leadership, today the Association for Consortium Leadership (ACL)—and he authored a definition that still has relevance today. According to Patterson (1970), academic consortia share five distinct characteristics. The consortia are

- Voluntary, not the result of regulatory or statutory mandate
- Multi-institutional, not merely bilateral agreements
- Multifunctional, not single-purpose
- Beneficiaries of long-term member support
- Managed by a substantial professional staff team

Academic consortia form for one simple reason: to serve their member institutions. Today, many consortia are highly specialized, focusing on one core area of cooperation such as library resource sharing or the joint purchasing of goods and services. Other consortia involve many offices and programs within their member institutions. Broadly stated, the mission of any consortium is to enable the members to achieve together, through cooperation, what cannot be achieved alone. A successful consortium supports its participants through shared risk and reward, at the same time strengthening the capacity of each partner college to pursue its unique institutional mission.

Experience shows that consortia do not form and survive easily. The culture and traditions of higher education have emphasized strict institutional autonomy. Most faculty are rewarded for independent effort, and colleges have focused on what distinguishes them from one another rather than on shared characteristics and needs. The 1990s, however, have introduced a new paradigm of organizational behavior that is characterized by cooperation, collaboration, and teamwork. The RAND report (Kaganoff, 1998) cites two studies, Baker (1993) and Tushnet (1993), which found several common factors in successful collaborations:

hared vision
'y defined goals
on real problems
'ionalized decision-making structure
'n making

- Continuity among partnership personnel
- Systematic communication with all partners and with the community
- Sufficient time for institutional change to occur
- The provision of resources to those whose roles and relationships will change
- The provision of professional development training

This chapter looks at academic consortia from the twin perspectives of a three-year-old consortium (Colleges of the Fenway), which is still in the process of being created, and a thirty-year-old consortium (Colleges of Worcester Consortium), which is in the midst of being re-created.

Motivations for Forming a Consortium

A 1991 survey of consortia in higher education conducted by the Association for Consortium Leadership (ACL) found that there were six common activities in which over 25 percent of all consortia engaged: cross-registration of students, faculty exchange, library cooperation, professional development (especially faculty development), workshops, and conferences. Also common among formal consortia are cooperative purchasing programs, the promotion of higher education, and outreach to public and private sector partners.

Academic enhancement through cross-registration, faculty exchanges, library cooperation, or joint academic programs is the single most common motivating factor for colleges to come together. The opportunity to achieve economies of scale and cost savings through nonduplication of services is another reason colleges have created consortia. Others have focused on bringing economic resources and public visibility to a geographic area or group of schools; in some cases, what began as informal relationships with volunteer cooperation has developed into formal agreements and leveraged support.

Once a consortium is formed, successful programming, the building of collegial relationships, and the opportunity to improve individual personnel performance all serve as motivators for sustaining the formal connection.

Colleges of the Fenway

Colleges of the Fenway is a three-year-old consortium established in 1995 in the Fenway area of Boston, Massachusetts. The institutional members include Emmanuel College, Massachusetts College of Pharmacy and Allied Health Sciences, Simmons College, Wentworth Institute of Technology, and Wheelock College. They came together under the vision and leadership of the five college presidents with three main goals: to enhance the academic environment and academic opportunities for students and faculty, to slow escalating costs through joint purchasing and the sharing of resources, and to retain their identities as small private colleges while offering the resource advantages of a much larger academic institution.

The first cooperative step these colleges took was to align their academic calendars and begin allowing students to cross-register at no additional charge. Soon afterward, counterparts across the institutions began to meet to explore other opportunities for collaboration. After developing an overlying set of "Principles of Collaboration," the presidents agreed to let ad hoc groups continue to meet to see what new initiatives might grow out of these conversations. Within the first year, admissions directors put together a joint recruitment brochure, and an annual guidance counselor tour was launched to bring high school guidance counselors to the schools. Further, an employment fair was created, and a new student health insurance vendor was selected, which achieved a significant reduction in the insurance premium for students. The initial principles fostered successful programs, which themselves have become motivators for looking at additional opportunities for collaboration.

As new consortia are forming, a key issue is what motivates each participating school to become involved in the relationship. Chief executive officers from different institutions may have very different reasons for believing that the alliance is strategically valuable. A clear vision for the consortium, identifiable goals, and a realistic assessment of what each institution is seeking to gain are vital for the success of the joint venture. For example, within the Colleges of the Fenway, two members do not offer foreign language courses. Consortium cross-registration has opened opportunities for foreign language study to these students.

Colleges of the Fenway is one of a handful of consortia in which the schools share geographic proximity. Close proximity can motivate colleges to look to neighboring institutions for solutions to common problems, and it can open opportunities for collaboration in areas such as shared facilities. The Colleges of Worcester Consortium (in Massachusetts), the Claremont Colleges (in California), and the Atlanta University Center represent several of the most established and integrated consortia that are among schools located in proximity to each other.

Geographic proximity can also make it easier to build the interpersonal relationships necessary for forming groups to have an identity as a consortium. Shared identity can become a key organizing element as the schools consider addressing concerns that relate to their geography. It can also help overcome whatever competition may exist.

Colleges of Worcester Consortium

The Colleges of Worcester Consortium, Inc., is a thirty-year-old association ʿolleges and universities in and around Worcester, Massachusetts. Memʾip includes Anna Maria College, Assumption College, Becker College, ʾniversity, College of the Holy Cross, Quinsigamond Community Colʾ University (through its School of Veterinary Medicine), the Uniʾssachusetts Medical Center, Worcester Polytechnic Institute, and ʾe College. The consortium grew out of conversations among the presidents of three of the founding members (Clark, Holy Cross, and Worcester Polytechnic Institute) during a stressful period of student unrest and the economic pressures of the late 1960s. It quickly became apparent to those presidents that a formal arrangement to support cooperation could provide advantages and enable a self-sustaining enterprise to emerge. Among the early efforts at cooperation were joint faculty development programs, joint community relations, and eventually the adoption of a preexisting, regional library cooperative.

Throughout its history, the Colleges of Worcester Consortium has developed a significant identity in the community and has created important programs in cross-registration and joint purchasing. It has served as the mechanism for serious conversations about the role of higher education in the local economy and has been called on from time to time to address public policy issues such as proposed local taxing of not-for-profit organizations.

With the retirement of a chief staff officer in 1995, the consortium board restated fundamental assumptions about the organization, modified its governing structure to involve vice-president-level executives in board discussions, and asserted three primary objectives for near-term development. Those objectives included additional academic cooperation, strengthened faculty development programming, and collaborative attention to the role of information and communication technology in higher education. With a renewed sense of focus, the consortium hired a new chief staff officer and embarked on a process of revitalizing the consortium.

Levels of Commitment and Involvement

As noted in the two examples cited earlier, executive-level institutional support is crucial to the overall success of a developing consortium and no less critical to successfully sustaining one. Presidential and senior-vice-presidential involvement gives the effort credibility within the member institutions and ensures that the organization keeps focused on strategically important issues. Further, structuring an effective consortium involves trust among the participants. Trust is a key factor if institutions are going to get beyond the marginal and project-oriented activities that make good public relations stories but are unlikely to have a lasting impact on members.

Successful consortia have a clear sense of mission and purpose. A written mission statement, or "Principles of Collaboration" as in the Colleges of the Fenway, sends a clear message to both internal and external communities about what motivates the schools to come together. Operational committees can use such a statement as a guide in considering new joint ventures. Consortium staff can use it as a tool by which to evaluate new ideas. The involvement of the senior administration will, de facto, define the depth and breadth of the collaboration. If the consortium is to have a strategically important role to play in the plans of the member colleges, participants must devote the time and energy necessary to come to an understanding of the potential of the group. Members must have a shared understanding of the goals and objectives of the organization, and measurable outcomes should be identified to ensure benefits to the members and success for the organization.

Further, there needs to be recognition of and a commitment to the extensive time it will take to develop joint programs and services. Joint activities will not come about if the effort is relegated to the corner of the desk. Working with a group takes time: working on a group project that needs to achieve the goals of several organizations simultaneously takes significantly more time. A clear vision of the goals of the joint enterprise and a determined commitment to the involvement necessary to achieve those goals are both vital if a consortium is to succeed.

Nevertheless, most consortium activities begin on a limited project basis. Therefore, it is vital that operational-level committees are given clear guidance and objectives and that they are empowered by their institutions and by the shared understanding about cooperation to make the necessary decisions to move a project forward. The need for clarity and empowerment is especially critical for groups with representatives from varying "levels" within the member organizations. For them, clear communication processes and decision-making authority are crucial at the outset.

Consorting can also expose any weaknesses in internal communications within member institutions. Committee members need to understand that they are representing their institution's and their particular areas of professional responsibility. They need to come to the consortium with an understanding of the needs and goals of their school, and they must be able to judge when consortium programs and services can respond to those needs or support those goals. Although communication across the consortium is crucial, effective communication within individual schools is also vital.

Organizational Structure

Building effective communications and accountability processes in a consortium presents the board and staff with a dilemma. Consortia are essentially voluntary associations. The vitality of the consortium is intimately related to the voluntary and actively self-interested participation of numerous parties. Discovering that self-interests across institutions are best served if the institutions work together captures the essence of a successful consortium program. But discovering shared self-interest and then acting on that discovery frequently requires a sustained effort on everyone's part, and it requires an institutionalized mechanism (the consortium). For consortia to endure, they cannot depend solely on the occasional, serendipitous discovery of shared self-interest among their members. Therefore, the dilemma is how to create sustainability and accountability within a framework that is essentially voluntary. A lot of institutional and individual goodwill and vision are crucial to effective "consorting."

Decision Making at Colleges of the Fenway

Colleges of the Fenway is still working on defining the most appropriate decision-making structure. From the outset, the presidents have demonstrated commitment and involvement with the consortium. They have met monthly for almost three years, as have separate committees of chief financial officers, chief academic officers, and deans of students. The colleges early committed funding to hire a coordinator, and both the presidents' and two of the vice presidents' groups have gone on day-long planning retreats. A structure with a steering committee and the aforementioned counterpart groups was put into place during the first three months of consortium operation.

As the consortium approaches its third anniversary, however, there is some question as to whether this is the most effective structure for the future. For example, a study of potential joint administrative opportunities conducted by outside consultants for Colleges of the Fenway highlighted the need for decision makers to be at the table when essential decisions are being developed and made. The need for this level of participation may lead to the creation of more short-term functional committees with chairs appointed from the senior administrative level, while the committees of senior-level administrators themselves will continue to meet. Clearly, each consortium needs to develop its own system for decision making and communication.

Decision Making at the Colleges of Worcester Consortium

During the thirty-year history of the Colleges of Worcester Consortium, presidential involvement has been a constant. What has evolved over time, however, is a gap between the executive levels of institutional leadership and the operational committees. This gap has produced two counterproductive results. First, board meetings became a series of status reports, frequently presented by consortium staff who naturally felt responsibility for and took ownership of the organization. Second, being somewhat remote from the seat of power and institutional decision making, the operational committees—whose members also felt a keen sense of responsibility and ownership—developed their own identity, ways of doing business, and sets of priorities.

The consortium board sought to remedy the situation by establishing vice-presidential-level committees (of academic, fiscal, and student affairs officers) to oversee the work of the operational committees. The chairs of these committees—a chief academic officer, a chief fiscal officer, and a chief student affairs officer—are formally included in board deliberations as nonvoting members. These changes are intended both to improve communication and accountability throughout the organization and to bring to bear on board deliberations the informed perspective of the three policy-level officers. This approach requires time and patience if it is to work effectively. The inherently complex nature of consortium programs involving so many institutions leaves no room for quick and easy management and decision-making processes.

Economics: Sustaining Consortia

When it comes to starting a consortium, numerous sources can help participants get the effort under way—private foundations, state and federal agencies, corporate philanthropies, to name a few. Sustaining a consortium, especially over an extended period of time, is more difficult; many consortia never survive the initial momentum of external, start-up funding.

Beyond program and service determination, sustaining a consortium is really a matter of clarifying goals and benefits and then fashioning an algorithm for the distribution of costs that is perceived to be fair and equitable to the paying customers. In distributing costs, simply tracking benefits and charging accordingly will not suffice. Many benefits are indirect or intangible. How does one know, for example, when an idea for cost saving or problem solving gleaned from a consortium meeting will affect the home campus? Further, how does one assess members on the basis of such serendipitous but potentially very significant consequences? Yet a significant value of consortia is just such results, coming from sustained conversations among peers over extended periods.

Benefits derived from consortium services will have varying value for participating colleges over time. When a college is undergoing an accreditation visit, the significance and impact of joint purchasing programs and shared library resources loom especially large. When philanthropic donors are looking for evidence that their largess will have significant impact, the opportunity to disseminate ideas and services through a consortium network can be most persuasive. Ongoing services and networking are important not only at key strategic times but at all times. However, the relative value of the consortium and of each of its individual programs and services will rise and fall as times and circumstances change and will be seen differently from the perspectives of different member colleges.

How then can one distribute the costs of consorting in ways that reflect fairness to the members, provide for the continuing health of the consortium, and ensure the continuation of benefits to members?

The straightforward calculation of objective benefits received from consortium programs and services, or the potential to receive such benefits, can place a heavy burden on one or a few partners. The member institution with the largest faculty or staff or full-time equivalent (FTE) student enrollment can end up supporting a disproportionate share of the overall costs of the organization. Faced with this set of concerns, the Colleges of Worcester Consortium recently conducted an informal Internet survey among consortia in the United States and found the following characteristics of their funding formulas:

The structure for dues and fees charges in consortia is a product of historical practice and the local sense of fairness.

Dues structures are rarely reviewed once established; the most common dues structure relates dues charges to institutional size.

Institutional size measures include size of budget, amount of state funding, or a measure of enrollment (usually FTE enrollment).

Institutional size reflects both capacity to pay and capacity to benefit from consortium activities.

Many consortia charge transaction-based fees for some services (for example, faculty development events).

Many consortia fund some services on an equal share basis, regardless of institutional size—however measured.

Every consortium has local factors that make its charging algorithm make sense. In few cases are these factors directly applicable to other consortia. However, it is crucial that whatever the formulas used, the distribution of costs should be based on a clearly articulated sense of the tangible and intangible benefits derived by the members, and the formula must be accepted as fair by the participants. In many cases, an approach analogous to our bicameral system of governing is adopted. This approach takes some proportion of the cost of a program or service and distributes it equally among the participating members, the way the senatorial representation is distributed in the federal government. The remainder of the cost is then distributed by some agreed-upon factor like FTE students or faculty—the way representation is determined in the U.S. House of Representatives. This approach has the virtue of acknowledging that all members benefit to some degree but that some benefit more than others.

Two principles of the economics of consorting that do apply across consortia are the leveraging of member payments against each other and the leveraging of overall member payments against those of associate or nonaffiliated organizations. Everyone benefits from the creation of a pool of resources, and the larger the pool (generally speaking) the greater the potential benefits.

Cost Sharing at Colleges of the Fenway. When the Colleges of the Fenway was established in 1995, each participating school agreed to commit an equal share toward the funding of a central staff person. Additional expenditures related to developing programs and services are divided between the schools on differing bases. Some programs have followed a transaction-based fee model: each school pays for the specific service it receives, and costs for others have been equally divided between the participants. However, a concern has arisen about how to access benefits and allocate costs in outsourcing some joint contracts. What cost burden is one to put on the relative size one institution brings to a joint contract? Does larger size entitle an institution to a disproportionate share of the savings benefits? Is it realistic to expect larger members to subsidize the participation of the smaller schools for a particular contract? or vice versa? Regardless of which methods are selected, consortium participants should be prepared to spend a significant amount of time determining equitable ways to share the costs of the collaboration.

Cost Sharing at the Colleges of Worcester Consortium. The Colleges of Worcester Consortium has a thirty-year history of closed governing membership limited to those colleges and universities located in the City of Worcester Massachusetts and contiguous towns. Although the benefits of membership have been substantial enough for the consortium to survive thirty years of continuous service, recent reexamination of consortium mission and programs led the board to redefine member expectations.

A thorough review of consortium services and charges revealed some interesting facts:

• Including the ten governing member colleges and universities, a total of 107 organizations (cultural organizations, service organizations, welfare organizations, and youth agencies) benefit from and support the consortium's programs and services in some way—for example, by participating in joint purchasing contracts or serving as locations for internship placements.
• The distribution of costs is heavily weighted toward the ten member colleges, and those institutions are almost exclusively responsible for the burden of the administrative overhead of the organization.
• Fees charged to members for consortium services are heavily weighted toward an equal shares approach, regardless of size of institution or capacity to benefit from the activity.

The participation of nonmember colleges and other not-for-profit organizations in consortium services testifies to their value. However, the subsidy of nonaffiliated organizations adds to the burden of the members, and it frequently develops without any clear rationale. Steps are now under way to create a more equitable distribution of service costs within the membership and between the member and nonaffiliated organizations. Formulas and strategies for the fair distribution of costs take into account the history of cooperation and certain factors, such as capacity to benefit, that should make the resulting charging algorithms more equitable without making them too burdensome on any one member or participant organization.

Complexity of Consortia

Consortia are, by definition, complex. The Patterson definition identifies two dimensions of this complexity in most consortia: multi-institutional membership and multifunctional services. Two institutions cooperating on a program or service—bilateral cooperation—can be relatively complex but when a third and then a fourth and a fifth institution are added to the mix, the complexity of decision making increases dramatically.

Complexity also arises from the multifunctional aspect of most consortia. A single-purpose consortium might be a research cooperative, a library cooperative, or a joint purchasing cooperative. These forms of cooperation, although they may involve institutional commitments in a technical sense, are programmatic cooperatives at the operational level. When multiple programs and services are involved in cooperation, and multiple offices on each campus must be represented, the cooperation is truly institutional. That is why institutional leadership involvement is crucial and why strategic decision making is necessary for optimum benefit. A consortium may be multifunctional, but it cannot be all things to all members. Strategic focus must be introduced.

Complexity also results from the political nature of every consortium action. The simplest decision is subject to the maximum possible scrutiny by numerous institutional agents who are operating from a multitude of institutional and interpersonal perspectives. To say simply that consortia are about consensus building is to understate the vulnerability of every decision to factors too numerous to estimate. Consortium staff frequently do not know why a program or service idea will not work despite apparently right timing, clear objectives, clear benefits, and adequate resources. Those conditions by themselves are necessary to make cooperation work but far from sufficient to ensure that cooperation will happen.

Professional staff with the skills and training to lead the cooperative effort further complicate an already complex situation. Cooperative efforts are seldom led in the traditional sense. They are achieved by a complicated process of cultivation and cross-validation, and they result from a consummate sense of timing. Underneath everything, cooperation is voluntary. Sometimes the cooperating institutions just do not want to cooperate.

Consequently, consortium decision structures need to provide a balance between the capacity to act with decisiveness and the capacity to sustain a decision process through long routes to a successful conclusion. It took one author of this chapter eight years to develop a consortium joint purchasing program. Until the very end of the process, the institutions simply were not ready to make a commitment—a commitment that, once made, produced major benefits and a basis for expanded cooperation with other not-for-profit organizations in the community.

Under these conditions, excellent communications are critical, and selecting capable staff helps ensure that communication will happen. It is almost universally accurate to say that the institutional members of academic consortia do not fully understand the nature and operations of the consortium. The broad purposes served by the consortium are somewhat remote from the daily experience and needs of most of these individuals. As a result, it is not unusual for consortium staff to have to justify repeatedly what the organization does, why it costs so much, and why the institutions should continue to support it.

Good communications can mitigate these problems, but good communications cost money and are not an immediate benefit producer. So capable staff are critical to maintaining valid consortium functions and keeping the realities of cooperation in the forefront of membership thought processes. Staff need to be skilled enough to ensure that the consortium delivers real benefits to the membership, patient enough to wait out the processes of decision making no matter how protracted, and sophisticated enough to know when intervention can be effective.

Staffing at Colleges of the Fenway. Colleges of the Fenway began with one staff person working out of the Medical, Academic, and Scientific Community Organization (MASCO) central office. MASCO, a nonprofit organization to which the Fenway colleges already belonged, provided administrative backup through a shared staff assistant and accounting services. After two and one-half years, the consortium member colleges agreed to increase the dedicated consortium staff to 2.5 FTE, and to retain the location and connection with MASCO. Since MASCO is a 501(c)(3) organization in its own right, and all the consortium colleges are also MASCO members, they have chosen not to incorporate the consortium separately at this time; rather, Colleges of the Fenway will continue as one of MASCO's departments. MASCO also offers many nonconsortium services to the colleges. The addition of the consortium staff has helped make MASCO more aware of the colleges' needs, and it has served to educate college staff about MASCO and the existing MASCO services they can access.

All five Colleges of the Fenway members are small private colleges. This does not reduce the complexity of the organization or the complexity of its decision-making processes. As with all consortia, decision-making structures need to be defined, new ideas need a forum for deliberation and assessment, and getting used to the concept of collaboration takes time and work. For institutions accustomed to thinking and operating on their own, understanding the subtleties and communication issues associated with a shared contract or joint initiative takes significant rethinking. Within the Colleges of the Fenway, some colleges have only limited staff time to devote to joint initiatives. The staffing lines are fairly lean, and chief financial officers can find it difficult to undertake several initiatives if they do not have anyone else to sit in on committee deliberations. Differences in reporting structures also make it difficult to determine who should sit on committees. For example, in some member schools, the information technology department reports through the financial administration; in others, it reports through academic affairs.

Limiting the consortium to a one- or two-person central staff can ensure that the consortium does not create an administrative structure that duplicates the colleges' administrations. The limited size of the consortium staff will force the members to prioritize projects and determine how many initiatives they can pursue realistically.

Staffing at the Colleges of Worcester Consortium. The Colleges of Worcester Consortium has ten member institutions and ninety-seven nongoverning partners. It employs twenty-two full- and part-time staff organized into five departments, and it manages twenty-one distinct program and service budgets. Within the operational structure, there are twenty-three representative committees with as few as eight and as many as forty organizations represented.

In part, the complexity of the organization is demonstrated by the diversity of the governing membership: one medical school, one school of veterinary medicine, one technical institute, one community college, one state college, one nondenominational liberal arts college, three undergraduate Catholic liberal arts colleges, and one comprehensive research university. This institutional diversity creates barriers to cooperation, but it also enables the consortium staff to promote cooperation with the confidence that there is very little head-to-head competition between or among members. The consortium expects to broaden its governing membership in the near future, both adding to the complexity of the organization and creating more opportunities for cooperation across subsets of the membership.

Over the past three years, the consortium has developed more specialized key staff roles: an information management specialist, a professional development specialist, and an operations manager. The consortium has also undertaken the standardization of fiscal management and operational processes, moving away from a system dependent on the understanding and memory of individuals and toward a system of guidelines and procedures. Although this set of changes has led to increased understanding of the consortium's role and its capacities, it has also raised concerns among constituents about the need for and the direction of change.

These concerns will be addressed in the future through the institution of a formal strategic planning process. The process will be broadly representative of internal and external constituencies, and it will reassert the central mission and core functions of the organization consistent with governing member needs and expectations. Resource allocation and staffing will be used to focus the programs and services of the organization in the strategic directions identified by the planning process.

The reestablishment of the core functions of the consortium and the allocation of resources to reflect those functions will not diminish the complexity of the organization or its decision processes. The intent is to provide a clearer framework for decision making and to ensure that, wherever possible, staff has optimum latitude to use the organization's resources to deliver prescribed benefits in a cost-effective manner.

A Third-Party Role for Consortia

An effective consortium serves as a neutral, third party that is charged with managing the overall cooperative venture. The consortium staff keep projects on track, offer a neutral and objective presence at meetings, and build consensus among the participants. This third party can be as modest as one part-time coordinator or as complex as a twenty-five person staff.

The consortium staff is responsible for putting the combined interests of the group ahead of individual interests, treating every institution as equal, and creating a level playing field for the discussion and debate of issues and programs. Staff also provide the mechanism through which goals are achieved. Their tasks can vary from scheduling meetings (no small undertaking) to developing vendor relationships and managing shared contracts. They might put together newsletters and offer faculty development workshops for participating institutions and the larger higher education community.

In most cases, consortium staff must accept that, for the participants, the consortium is a low priority in the context of campus issues and day-to-day job responsibilities; yet staff must help keep consortium groups focused and on task. The consortium staff also provide stability in the face of staff turnover on the campuses; they provide continuity to the effort and are there to orient new representatives of member institutions.

Ideally, the consortium office will be a safe place for idea exploration and problem solving. The role of the staff is to facilitate the building of relationships and trust so that the true potential of the consortium can be realized; its role is also to serve as a buffer when trust is not achievable. Building trust and a team approach is crucial, takes time and energy, and can be quickly dismantled, especially by misplaced comments by those who are not willing to invest in the group. The staff's role is to foster such trust and to serve as a buffer when trust is not achievable.

While providing leadership for some cooperative efforts, consortium staff members also identify and support leaders among the institutional representatives. A consortium is foremost for and about the members and, as such, will assist them in finding new ways to address issues that are central to higher education.

The Importance of Continuity

Of the ten college and university presidents who constitute the board of the Colleges of Worcester Consortium, seven are new within the past three years. Some of the new institutional CEOs come to their positions with prior experience governing academic consortia; some do not. Among the vice presidential leadership in these institutions and among the representatives on operating committees, similar but not so dramatic turnover also has occurred. Therefore, the continuity of programs and services and the continuation of new directions for strategic development of the organization depend significantly on the capabilities of the consortium staff. Not only do staff hold a neutral, third-party perspective on the organization and its functions but they also provide a source of institutional memory to ensure continuity and focus for the overall effort.

Staff also provide links to other consortia and to professional organizations that serve as sources of ideas and experience valuable to the consortium effort. Through groups such as the Association for Consortium Leadership and the Professional and Organizational Development Network, staff are able to keep current on the development of programs and services that might be adapted to local conditions and responsive to local needs. Through recently developed listserves, consortium staff stay in touch with counterparts around the country and constantly test ideas and seek solutions to local problems from a far-ranging network of experienced colleagues.

Given the diversity of institutional types in the consortium, the staff has worked purposely to pull down barriers to cooperation and to identify programs and services of broad benefit. Staff also realize that cooperation can develop among subsets of the total membership. Larger membership, more partnerships among affiliated and nonaffiliated organizations, and the development of limited partnerships with the consortium framework are all ways that staff can ensure the largest return to each institution for each dollar and hour of staff time invested.

Conclusion

Starting an academic consortium is a serious undertaking. Sustaining a consortium is every bit as serious and much more complex. As the past thirty years have demonstrated, the enthusiasm and expectations that accompany new cooperative ventures frequently do not endure over time, and neither do the organizational forms that embody them.

Following is a summary of key elements that, in the experience of these authors and others (Medical, Academic, and Scientific Community Organization, 1997; Technical Development Corporation, 1998), contribute to the initial success and long-term sustainability of academic consortia:

- Leadership and commitment from the highest level
- A clear mission and goals
- Balance mechanisms for providing parity between the "heavy weights" and others
- Commitment and buy-in to the process by all parties
- Decision-making ability
- Neutral, third-party function
- Funding for the initial effort and an ability to make key investments when the collaboration requires it
- Clear agreements regarding cost-sharing arrangements
- Mechanisms for measuring success
- Effective structures and systems for communication among collaborators and within each college
- The flexibility to be nimble and creative; the ability to be experimental and to develop innovative pilot programs beyond member organizations' individual capacities

References

Baker, L. M. "Promoting Success in Educational Partnerships Involving Technology." In *Proceedings of Selected Research and Development Presentations,* Convention of the Association for Educational Communications and Technology, Research and Theory Division, New Orleans, La., Jan. 13–17, 1993.

Kaganoff, T. *Collaboration, Technology, and Outsourcing Initiatives in Higher Education: A Literature Review.* A report prepared by RAND for the Foundation for Independent Higher Education, 1998.

Medical, Academic, and Scientific Community Organization. *Briefing Document Outline,* Oct. 1997. Boston: Medical, Academic, and Scientific Community Organization.

Patterson, L. D. *Consortia in American Higher Education.* Washington, D.C.: ERIC Clearinghouse on Higher Education, November 1970.

Technical Development Corporation. *The Colleges of the Fenway Collaboration: A Report on Lessons Learned and a Model for Future Cooperation,* 1998.

Tushnet, N. C. *A Guide to Developing Educational Partnerships.* Washington, D.C.: Office of Educational Research and Improvement; Los Alamitos, Ca.: Southwest Regional Lab., Program for the Improvement of Practice, 1993.

FREDERICK BAUS *is executive director of the Colleges of Worcester Consortium, Worcester, Massachusetts.*

CLAIRE A. RAMSBOTTOM *is coordinator of the Colleges of the Fenway, Boston, Massachusetts.*

A consortium director must be a strong leader, whose primary duties range from providing leadership to securing resources to clearly communicating a consortium's mission.

The Role of the Consortium Director

Thomas R. Horgan

The academic consortium director's role is best described as a case study in dual leadership, with the director serving both as an arbitrator of the status quo and as a visionary of collaborative potentiality. Those who serve in this unique position quickly realize that it is a responsibility requiring talents ranging from the intellectual to the spiritual. Also they find it to be a role in which success is measured as much by the director's ability to move groups of academics in incremental steps as it is by the ability to initiate monumental accomplishments.

In examining the role of the consortium director, one must also examine the key elements found in successful consortial organizations. In general, a successful academic consortium can be characterized by a few identifiable indicators, including a board committed to the success of the organization, a clearly defined mission easily understood by various campus and noncampus constituencies, a stable operating budget and stream of revenue, and a strong, consistent, organizational leadership over a number of years.

Later in this chapter, I will examine the role of the consortium director as a leader and attempt to identify how this position affects the overall operations and success of an academic consortium. First, however, let us briefly review the other elements of successful consortium operations to better understand the director's role.

Board Support

The level of success any organization achieves, be it for-profit or not-for-profit, is directly tied to the level and quality of support provided by its board. This is particularly true in any academic consortium arrangement in which the board is often directly invested in activities and financially connected to the organization. Academic consortia existing by their very mission to serve member institutions are closely linked to board members who represent those same institutions. Therefore, for a consortium to succeed, board members must fully comprehend and support the mission and objectives of the consortium. This means board members must be willing to give both time and mind, in addition to their name, to ensure the consortium's success.

If board members want a consortium organization to succeed and grow, they must always undertake the actions necessary to ensure that strong organizational direction and leadership is in place and to supply the resources and encouragement that will ensure continued growth and success. This support must be broadly communicated by board members to the consortium's various campus constituencies, including both administrators and faculty members when appropriate, and to other community constituencies. Without visible support from board members, it will be problematic for a consortium to meet even its basic objective of service and collaboration. Only with strong support from board members can the promise of innovative new initiatives and renewal of the organization be anticipated and accomplished.

As a director of an academic consortium, I have observed first-hand the importance of board support for collaborative efforts and the lack of progress that occurs when board members are less than enthusiastic about particular initiatives. When the New Hampshire College and University Council's (NHCUC) board agreed to institute an annual academic affairs conference, they sent a strong message to deans and faculty that this should occur by designing the first colloquium themselves and then handing it off to a committee for future implementation. Today, the NHCUC hosts an annual academic affairs conference with a national speaker and over 250 participants. Alternatively, in attempts to form joint purchasing agreements among institutions, board members voice support for such efforts but have been unwilling and uninterested in moving these initiatives forward on their campuses. Subsequently, few tangible results have been achieved over the years, despite significant staff time and energy being put forward to promote the concept. Ultimately, a consortium director's efforts can only succeed if the board is committed to the consortium's work and the direction is empowered with board support.

Unfortunately, it is common for board members to find themselves involved in consortial arrangements established by their predecessors. Thus their personal commitment to the consortium's mission can range from mild disinterest to open hostility. This range of personal commitment highlights why it is important for consortium directors to do everything possible to bring new board members into the fold early and to lead new members to commit to the mission and purpose of the organization as early as possible. Obtaining additional assistance from current, supportive board members is an effective resource in building this affinity, as does finding an activity that is of particular interest to the new member. When presidential colleagues appear convinced that taking an active role in consortial activities is beneficial to their institutions, new members are much more likely to give serious attention to their role as board members as well. At the New Hampshire College and University Council we have learned the benefits from making early visits to the campus office of new board members to establish an initial positive link with the consortium. It is self-evident that spending an appropriate amount of time seeking multiple ways to engage board member is always a good investment. Conversely, neglecting board development and cultivation is always done at the director's peril and will, in most instances, end badly for all involved.

Clearly Defined Mission

When asked if they understand the mission of a particular consortium, most respondents will reply with a statement that reflects the particular segment of the mission that they are personally connected with or feel comfortable expressing. Generally these explanations are at best incomplete and at times misguided. This blurred vision of a consortium's mission should always be monitored by directors for opportunities to clarify it, even while recognizing that it most often occurs when a consortium serves multiple purposes and diverse constituencies.

The New Hampshire College and University Council provides an example of a consortium engaged in a wide range of consortial projects, including admissions, library collaboration, career services, academic cooperation, advocacy, and community service. While the council has responsibilities for each of these diverse activities (and several additional programs under our broadly crafted mission statement), it is not unusual to hear the NHCUC's mission narrowly defined only in light of one or two of these purposes. "The NHCUC is a consortium for sharing library resources," or "The Council is that group that works on admissions projects for the four-year colleges" are common descriptions of our work. Although these singular definitions are not inaccurate, they are so narrow in scope as to give a very incomplete perception of the consortium's purpose or ongoing activities. It is critically important that directors strive to ensure that a definitive understanding of the consortium's work is in place and that it is expressed in as many and varied venues as possible. This should be accomplished both in an effort to increase the clearest possible understanding of the consortium's mission and to ensure that the consortium's purposes are comprehended fully.

Defining and ensuring that the mission is broadly understood may be the most significant responsibility of any consortium director. Without this broad-based understanding, it is nearly impossible to collect critical support for any consortial activity. At the NHCUC, this vision is accomplished through regular board and committee meetings, through publications and, significantly, through the development of a strategic plan designed with the member college presidents. This effort to set a strategic plan in place should be seriously undertaken and renewed every few years to re-affirm the direction in which the consortium is moving and to ensure that board members are in concert with the direction and objectives of the consortium.

Once a strategic plan is in place, the director has a working document to use as the cornerstone for building all consortium activities. This document also serves as a useful vehicle for outlining the mission of the organization for both internal and external constituencies. In truth, it is very difficult to get a board motivated to undertake a strategic planning process, especially when things are perceived to be going smoothly. However, it is generally the first action the board will undertake when things are going badly. Thus, moving this action item forward will consistently fall to the director, who should recognize that a strategic plan assists in avoiding some of the basic pitfalls confronting all organizations.

Stable Operating Budgets and Streams of Revenue

Establishing operating budgets that provide needed resources to undertake successfully the mission of a consortium is another critical factor requiring the direct attention of the director. The director will almost always be held accountable for developing the annual operating budget for board approval and for balancing accounts at the end of each fiscal year. Many directors find this to be the most tedious of tasks and will go to great lengths to avoid having to "look at the numbers." However, taking a firm hand in developing the consortium's operating budget and making certain that the organization is living within its projected revenues and expenses will be beneficial in establishing the respect and trust of board members, as well as other constituents, in the management of the consortium. It is an unusual board that wants to be involved in the financial micromanagement of the consortium, and the director will be best served by performing this duty in a professional and efficient manner on their behalf.

The other side of the financial picture (apart from budget formation) involves securing a steady stream of revenue for the organization. This is a key component in the director's role as the chief financial officer for the consortium. Many an organization flounders on the shoals of under-funding and ultimately collapses due to poor budgetary controls, inadequate financial planning, and uncertain financial resources. This scenario can only be avoided if the director develops skills to manage the consortium within the parameters established in its mission statement and strategic plan, and works with the board to establish realistic revenue sources to secure the financial future. Once the board has identified the specific goals of the organization, in consultation with the director, it can then undertake the important annual work of building a budget and determining how resources will be secured.

Recently, the NHCUC participated in the formation of an affiliate state organization of the national organization of *Campus Compact* and effectively implemented this process of first identifying goals, creating a budget, and then planning ways to meet the financial requirements to fulfill the mission. The board was then actively invested in securing the funds to meet the goals of the organization. Academic consortia often raise a significant amount of their annual operating budgets through member assessments or other member fees. However, with increasingly limited budgets and declining resources available from most higher education institutions, academic consortia must strive to identify outside revenue sources to meet specific programmatic needs. A word of caution to directors: this must always be done in close consultation with your board and with full board support for success to be achieved. It is a reality that consortium board members will always be torn between the general good of the consortium and their own institutional self-interest. Therefore, all external fundraising must be done in full recognition of this natural conflict and be worked out well in advance of any fundraising requests being made.

Indeed, the NHCUC has successfully moved from nearly total reliance on member assessments for annual operating expenses five years ago to about one-third of operating funds now generated through member assessments. This was accomplished by obtaining board support to identify outside grant funding opportunities in a manner that did not conflict with member institutions' own fundraising objectives. Federal grants and regional and national foundations can play a significant role in providing such alternative funding.

Strong Organizational Leadership

When any organization begins the process of searching for a new executive director, it usually begins with the goal of finding a "strong leader." Any cursory review of the *Chronicle of Higher Education's* "Bulletin Board" of available positions for consortial positions reveals some of the common jargon associated with the search for a new leader. Frequently cited terms include "someone who will move the organization forward," or "someone who inspires confidence," or "someone who has the ability to identify opportunities and resources to promote the organization." All are admirable traits. However, clearly defining necessary leadership traits and knowing them when you see them are difficult tasks. Ultimately, whether the position is for a college president, a corporate CEO, or a consortium director, boards most often are looking for a good manager. This is particularly true in the academic consortium world, as college presidents have little time or inclination to manage the operations of a consortium in addition to their own institutional operations. The board most likely desires someone to ensure that the day-to-day operations of the consortium are being handled smoothly and professionally. Once the board becomes comfortable with the management it has put in place, it will increasingly be inclined to support movements into new initiatives, which require real leadership skills from the consortium director. At this point, the director must be prepared to provide both creative management and show true visionary leadership.

It is critical then that the consortium director first demonstrate real management ability and then use leadership skills in arenas where significant change can be achieved. At the NHCUC, this has been accomplished by generating renewed consortial activity that provides a sense of substantial activity occurring, while simultaneously moving the council into new areas of activity engaging the board and generating support for further consortial responsibilities.

Putting It All Together

Interinstitutional cooperation among academic institutions is both ripe with possibilities and brimming with potential pitfalls. With the internal and external pressures facing higher education institutions to reduce costs and simultaneously increase access and ensure quality, an increasing emphasis on collaborative initiatives is likely to occur over the next several years. Indeed, Congress has recently called for greater collegial efficiencies and collaboration in their *National Commission on the Cost of Higher Education Report.*

At the same time, competitiveness among institutions is as prevalent today as at any time in the history of higher education and is a major block to full consortial collaboration. Thus it is only through a sustained convergence of collaborative institutional interests, coupled with strong board support, clearly defined missions, sustained funding, and strong organizational leadership, that the consortium director can hope to achieve significant success.

When left to their own devices, higher education institutions most naturally regress to their own singular self-interest. In reality, this may often be best for their individual institutional objectives. It is only when the consortium director can identify collaborative projects that are feasible, significant, and efficient that the role of the director becomes meaningful to institutions.

Key Elements in the Director's Role

A consortium director plays a unique role in the lives of the consortium's membership. He or she must be both a leader and a servant. The director must know how to use a college president's time wisely and how to serve as an advocate in a variety of settings. The director must also help presidents recognize their potential to advance their cause in a united fashion. Therefore, the work of the director must be purposeful and respectful of the varied needs, expectations, and missions of the institutions, and make adjustments accordingly. It is an all-too-common error to expect each president or institution to respond to consortium proposals or initiatives with equal enthusiasm. If the director is mindful of these differences, the right balance between total member involvement and occasional indifference can be achieved. In the process, the director will gain the respect of the presidents for recognizing these differences.

Ultimately, the director must keep in mind that the work of the consortium is valuable only to the degree that it eases the load on the individual member institutions and enhances their collective efforts. Initiatives must readily appear to be of clear value to the participating institutions and provide efficiencies and cost savings that could not be accomplished alone. When a consortium director discovers the proper balance between institutional self-interest and collaborative cooperation, the strategic role of the director in promoting alliances becomes evident. It is this discovery of the potentiality of interinstitutional collaboration that ultimately drives institutions to work in consort.

THOMAS R. HORGAN is executive director of the New Hampshire College and University Council, Bedford, New Hampshire.

College and university libraries can work together to enhance library access and share resources, but the problems inherent in forging such alliances will not be easily solved.

Library Cooperation

Neil R. Wylie, Tamara L. Yeager

This chapter was not written by librarians or for librarians. Rather it was written by two consortium directors for other consortium directors whose institutional members are considering library cooperation. One of us serves a consortium with a long history of library cooperation in a state where a central library system is operating successfully. The other serves a consortium in which the head librarians from the land-grant universities in six different states are trying to find the common ground for meaningful cooperation.

It ought to be easy for librarians to forge new library alliances. They have been laying the groundwork for many years, as they have been developing and adopting common standards for cataloguing library materials. After cataloguing systems, the most common example of cooperation is probably interlibrary loans, which are available from virtually any public and most private libraries in the United States. When requesting materials from other libraries, librarians rely most often for availability information from OCLC, an Ohio-based nonprofit corporation that began in 1967 and evolved from the original Ohio College Library Center to become the OCLC Online Computer Library Center, Inc., serving libraries throughout the world. Although delivery of interlibrary loan materials typically takes several days, new library software systems make it possible to markedly reduce the time required.

Existing library consortia illustrate some important considerations for forming a new library consortium. Most are limited to the confines of a single state or to a subset of libraries within a state, such as a higher education system, or to a group of libraries that are located in the same metropolitan community. Examples include the GALILEO system in Georgia, OhioLINK in Ohio, VIVA in Virginia, PORTALS in Oregon, and CLICnet in Minnesota. State library systems often receive funding earmarked for collaboration.

NEW DIRECTIONS FOR HIGHER EDUCATION, no. 106, Summer 1999 © Jossey-Bass Publishers

When libraries are not all located within the same major governmental or administrative unit, organizational processes become more complex and funding more problematic. Nevertheless, successful multistate library consortia are beginning to emerge, including SoliNET in the southeastern United States and the CIC Virtual Electronic Network in the Midwest. Other interstate library consortia are in the planning or early implementation stages, including the Big 12 Plus Library Consortium and the New England land-grant university libraries. A relatively new organization, the International Coalition of Library Consortia, attempts to monitor and coordinate the activities of library consortia.

Library catalogue automation has progressed to the point that most college and university libraries make it possible to search for materials through on-line public access catalogues. If all libraries in a consortium use the same public catalogue software, it can be easy to display holdings from several libraries concurrently, as if all the materials were held by the same library. However, there are several different vendors of library automation software, and linkage of their proprietary systems is difficult.

An international standard, Z39.50, is being developed to overcome the incompatibilities associated with different library automation software, but so far, having the standard has not meant that the problem is solved. No vendor has yet adopted the Z39.50 standard as the basis for its own library automation system.

The New England Land-Grant University Libraries

When the directors and deans of the six New England land-grant university libraries began in 1995 to seriously discuss possibilities for greater coordination of their activities, the potential seemed almost unlimited. After a goal-setting workshop in the fall of 1997, this vision emerged:

> A consortial relationship will be established in which: the collaborative effort strengthens each library's ability to support the mission of its home institution, technology is used to enhance the utility and utilization of the collection, faculty and students from member institutions are viewed as the clients of all libraries, the collective negotiates most favorable monetary and service terms with vendors, the staffs of the several libraries work synergistically resulting in both local and consortial benefit, innovation is enhanced through collective action and shared risk, and the benefits of our collaborative efforts are recognized and supported by our institutional and community leaders.

The vision seems clear, but it has taken until now to discover and begin to sort through the details necessary for implementation. The libraries have made, and are continuing to make, important discoveries about themselves because of the process. They've made discoveries about their institutions, their relationships to one another, the marketplace, and the promise and reality of emerging digital technologies.

The New England land-grant libraries are located in six different states, and no central authority or agency beyond the universities themselves has either encouraged collaboration or guaranteed short- or long-term funding. Outside funding sources are being investigated that may help implement specific project elements, but winning outside funding for the entire project seems unlikely. In this environment, without outside mediating or energizing forces and without the promise of outside funding, all challenges and institutional differences are amplified.

One of the most frustrating concerns expressed during the consortium planning process was whether the land-grant university libraries in New England were the right partners. Although they all share flagship public research university and land-grant status within their states, the universities vary in size and reputation. Student enrollment ranges from approximately eight thousand to approximately twenty-two thousand, and library holdings and other tangible resources generally mirror those differences. Although they are all relatively small institutions by flag-ship state university standards, the combined holdings of print materials by the six libraries equal or exceed the holdings of any of the top research libraries in the United States. The possibility of creating that combined collection has kept people from all six institutions interested in pursuing the project.

Consistent with their vision of collaboration, the New England land-grant directors and deans of libraries have identified six major areas where the potential benefits of collaboration should be fully explored. The possible benefits of each may seem obvious, but barriers have been identified for every one.

Sharing Print Collections. Technology exists to create a virtual union catalogue, and that, coupled with a state-of-the-art user-initiated interlibrary loan and document delivery system, would significantly benefit users of library materials. Unless holdings of the consortium libraries can be displayed concurrently, user-initiated interlibrary loans from other cooperating libraries probably are not possible.

We believe the processing and delivery of interlibrary loan materials can be expedited to the point where delivery of materials in less than forty-eight hours is the norm. In addition to being a timesaving convenience to borrowers, user-initiated interlibrary loans also benefit the libraries. Professional staff members are not needed to monitor and process the loan transactions. Balancing loan activity among the libraries so that excessive requests do not place an unfair burden on any is simplified.

Because the six New England land-grant university libraries use library automation software from several vendors, a Z39.50 or similar solution is required to create a virtual union catalogue. Some of the libraries are unwilling to commit to Z39.50 at this time, but one subgroup uses an automation system that permits easy linkages to similar systems, and it has decided to implement user-initiated interlibrary loans. Other libraries will be welcome to join when linkage to their own proprietary systems becomes less difficult. Although not all six libraries will directly benefit at the beginning, the cooperating libraries will begin to demonstrate the tangible benefits of collaboration among land-grant university libraries in New England, and the nonparticipating libraries have supported this step.

In addition to enabling user-initiated interlibrary loans, a virtual union catalogue also makes it possible to achieve greater coordination of library collections. Library staff members will work together to reduce collection overlap in targeted areas and redirect freed resources to strengthen other areas.

Sharing Electronic Information. The New England land-grant librarians have conceived of an electronic gateway to the collections of all the libraries over which digital resources could be shared. The full text of many professional journals is now available in electronic format, for example, and the journals can be licensed so that access by legitimate users of any of the consortium libraries is permitted.

Publishers of electronic journals have been reluctant to consider new policies that would encourage the greater use of electronic formats. Although we originally thought cost savings would be possible by using common points of access to digital information, significant savings will not be achieved unless the pricing policies of publishers change or other groups of academic professionals begin to create their own digital publications.

Several of the New England land-grant libraries are repositories for federal documents and publications, and it is increasingly difficult to keep all of them accessible to the public. Using an electronic gateway, a more effective shared system can be developed and duplicate copies of little-used materials can be avoided. Access to all federal documents can be improved, while reducing the storage and retrieval burdens on individual libraries.

Sharing Library Staffs. All of the projects under consideration by the New England land-grant librarians will require the cooperation of staff members from all six of the libraries. This will require trust in the professional capabilities and judgments of one another that cannot be assumed to exist now, and meetings of staff members with relevant expertise and responsibilities are being built into all of the projects being designed under this consortium initiative. Travel costs will be significant, and travel to meetings will need to be supplemented and eventually supplanted by teleconferences, audioconferences, and electronic e-mail discussions.

Collaboratively Developing a New England Learning Community. Because their universities are the historic home to the public colleges of agriculture and engineering in their states and are also home to cooperative extension and the agricultural research experiment stations, it is natural for land-grant university librarians to extend their service concerns to the learning and information needs of every citizen. They plan to create an open-information access and referral system, where the six New England land-grant university libraries serve as the principal information nodes for their states' and the rest of New England's citizens. Other libraries will be encouraged to join the consortium and add their resources through the consortium network. Thus, any citizen in any of the six states will have access through local libraries to library materials available anywhere in the region. Not only will traditional students benefit but adults in continuing education programs, other adults pursuing lifelong learning goals, not-for-profit organizations, state and local governmental units, and large and small businesses will benefit as well.

Collaboratively Creating a New England Digital Library. Using a shared digital gateway, it will be possible for users to access any of the unique materials held in digital format by any of the libraries. A center for digitization is proposed to transform existing materials into digital representations, but the librarians have not yet faced the question of where it will be. Included, in addition to printed materials, will be handwritten letters and manuscripts, musical recordings, photographs, and motion pictures.

New search and retrieval tools may be created to serve digital libraries, and the librarians have recently endorsed a grant proposal to create a system to search for and retrieve materials by appearance (handwritten works, photographic images, architectural forms, and so forth). Another grant application to develop methods for preserving digital materials is being developed.

Creating and Taking Advantage of an Enhanced Information Infrastructure. All the librarians recognize that the existing Internet configuration in New England will be inadequate to serve the long-term aspirations of the New England library consortium they envision. However, the Internet 2 system, plus the promise of the federal Next Generation Internet initiative, together create the expectation that sufficient bandwidth will be available to serve as substrate to the projects described. Three of our librarians either are now serving or have served as their institution's chief technology or information officer. Their knowledge of and involvement in their university's broader information planning efforts will help ensure that the bandwidth needs of the libraries are met.

Obviously, the difficulties of creating and promoting library cooperation among institutions in several states present problems not easily solved. In fact, getting institutions to agree to the use of software that will facilitate the sharing of catalogue information is challenging among institutions with a history of working together, that is, similar types of institutions or institutions in a single state.

Ohio Library and Information Network, OhioLINK

Ohio has a long history of higher education consortia work. The Ohio College Association is one of the oldest consortia in the United States and is still active in promoting the collaboration of the higher education community in Ohio. Ohio is also the founding home of both OCLC and more recently OhioLINK.

The Ohio Library and Information Network, OhioLINK, is a consortium of Ohio's colleges and universities and the State Library of Ohio. OhioLINK serves more than five hundred thousand students, faculty, and staff at seventy-four institutions and offers access to more than twenty-four million library items statewide. It also provides access to sixty-seven research databases, including a variety of full-text resources.

OhioLINK offers user-initiated on-line borrowing through a statewide central catalogue. It also provides a delivery service among member institutions to speed the exchange of library items. To date, the OhioLINK central catalogue contains almost seven million master records from its seventy-four institutions, encompassing a spectrum of library material including law, medicine, and special collections. In addition to the central catalogue, users can access sixty-seven electronic research databases covering a variety of disciplines. OhioLINK's full-text resources include on-line encyclopedias, dictionaries, literature, and journal articles.

OhioLINK serves faculty, students, staff, and other resources at member institutions via campus library systems, campus networks, and the Internet. The system provides access to more than 4,500 simultaneous users at 113 locations, serving more than 500,000 patrons. The OhioLINK central catalogue also is available to outside users through the Internet. However, access to the research databases is restricted to OhioLINK member users (valid patrons at OhioLINK member institutions). OhioLINK's membership includes seventeen public universities, twenty-three community or technical colleges, thirty-three private colleges, and the State Library of Ohio.

OhioLINK is part of the ongoing tradition in pioneering library automation in Ohio. The Ohio State University and others in Ohio began integrating campus library systems at an early date. In the 1960s, state funds supported the development of OCLC, then called the Ohio College Library Center. OCLC has since grown into an international organization with a database of thirty million entries representing materials held in more than ten thousand libraries. The private sector in Ohio also has been actively involved in library automation. Organizations such as LEXIS-NEXIS, OhioNET, and Chemical Abstract Services continue to develop and provide new products and services to the nation's libraries. OhioLINK is working with many of these organizations to expand the services it provides to users.

Southwestern Ohio Council for Higher Education Library Cooperation

The Southwestern Ohio Council for Higher Education (SOCHE) was founded in 1967 to promote interinstitutional cooperation and community service, which leads to educational advancement in the region, research development of common interest to its members, and the administrative efficiency of the member institutions. The vision of the consortium is to be a catalyst for regional educational cooperation that aggressively promotes the sharing of resources and expertise among its institutional members to strengthen their economic and cultural communities. In 1996, SOCHE adopted Albert Einstein's statement: "No problem can be solved from the same consciousness that created it. We must learn to see the world anew."

The SOCHE Library Council also has a long history of interinstitutional cooperation. For many years, the consortium office managed a van delivery system for its members to share library resources. This system was operated until 1995 when the inception of the OhioLINK delivery system was initiated. Currently, most SOCHE institutions are members of OhioLINK, and all are able to use the delivery service to move resources among the membership.

Recently revised, the mission of the Library Council of the Southwestern Ohio Council for Higher Education is to promote and enhance access to information and library resources for the constituencies of participating institutions. Contributing as partners to cooperative activities that improve services beyond the abilities of any single institution, the members commit to the following four goals: (1) creating professional development opportunities for all levels of library staff and facilitating interlibrary communication and collaboration, (2) sharing expertise and resources to support common information needs, (3) supporting activities and programs that enhance the role of the library in the academic community, and (4) promoting and supporting library service assessment activities. In order to direct the energies of the Library Council and the SOCHE staff, objectives and strategies for each goal were developed.

Goal 1. *Objective 1:* To provide a variety of training and professional development opportunities consistent with the needs of all levels of member library staffs. Strategies include

Planning and scheduling regular program meetings addressing a wide range of library issues.

Developing III and OhioLINK training and advancement programs using member library personnel because almost all member libraries have a common technological core in Innovative Interfaces and OhioLINK.

Establishing user groups among member library staffs where common systems and resources have broad operational impact (for example, Innovative Interfaces and OhioLINK software systems).

Objective 2: To facilitate formal and informal communication among member libraries. Strategies include

Preparing and maintaining library staff directories of member institutions.

Participating and encouraging participation as appropriate in electronic communication (for example, via listserves).

Creating interest groups where and when appropriate to encourage informal communication.

Objective 3: To ensure that member library staffs are informed about available training opportunities in the region and to coordinate participation where appropriate. Strategies include

Supporting electronic communication, via the library staff listserve.

Objective 4: To maintain an organizational structure that will facilitate interaction and the development and implementation of cooperative efforts. Strategies include

Appointing committees, task groups, and interest groups deemed appropriate to accomplish the current strategies of the council.

Goal 2.

Objective 1: To identify available staff and information resources and services within member institutions. Strategies include preparing, maintaining, and distributing service directories and developing databases of unique library resources available in member institution libraries.

Objective 2: To expedite the transfer of information and resource materials to patrons. Strategies include participating fully in the OhioLINK PCirc direct borrowing program; providing interlibrary loan services at no charge to member institutions; sharing media resources for faculty use and at no charge to member institutions; providing printed reminders, for distribution to library users, of the services of member institution libraries (for example, Bookmark).

Objective 3: To develop structures and procedures to support cooperative efforts in sharing staff expertise.

Objective 4: To promote and support member library participation in the OhioLINK library system while maintaining Council support for those member libraries not able to participate.

Objective 5. To explore possible cooperative collection development initiatives.

Goal 3.

Objective 1: To assist in promoting the role of the Library in the academic community. Strategies include developing faculty and administrative forums on the changing information technology environment and the progressive present and future responses and roles of libraries; sponsoring learning forums that assist library users, especially faculty, in coping with the complicated information environments (for example, copyright, information technology resources); supporting the development of library advocacy groups on the campuses of member institutions (for example, Friends of the Library).

Objective 2: To broaden awareness in constituent communities of SOCHE Library Council Activities.

Objective 3: To develop collective policies for responding to the service needs of common constituencies.

Objective 4: To foster the examination and discussion of library issues and trends within the SOCHE library community and among the broader academic community.

Goal 4.

Objective 1: To share assessment techniques and expertise. Strategies include serving as a clearinghouse for the identification of the best assessment tools for measuring library effectiveness; providing training in the effective use of Innovative Interfaces and OhioLINK statistical capabilities in assessment activities.

Objective 2: To be cooperative, where appropriate, in consortiumwide assessment activities to measure the impact and success of library services.

Objective 3: To present the value and quality of member library resources and services as a regional asset.

Conclusion

The future of SOCHE library cooperation is best characterized as a movement from the sharing of "things" to the sharing of "people and expertise." This is possible because of the current environment for sharing traditional library resources. The library council is actively seeking ways to become more intrinsically involved in the discussions and plans of teaching, learning, and technology initiatives. They are also in the process of identifying joint projects with the SOCHE Council of Chief Academic Officers. Finally, the library directors are developing a leadership program that focuses on the future of librarianship and fosters conversations on the directions of libraries and resource sharing.

More information about the organizations mentioned in this chapter may be found on the World Wide Web. Information about SOCHE may be obtained at [www.soche.org]. Connect with [www.oclc.org] for information about OCLC and with [www.ohiolink.edu] for more information about OhioLINK. Information about the Council of Presidents, New England Land-Grant Universities may be found at [www.necop.org].

NEIL R. WYLIE is the executive officer of the New England Land-Grant Universities Council of Presidents in Durham, New Hampshire.

TAMARA L. YEAGER is executive director of Southwestern Ohio Council for Higher Education in Dayton, Ohio.

Cross-registration systems and joint academic programs create a variety of educational opportunities for students and provide many benefits to a consortium's member institutions.

Cross-Registration and Joint Academic Programs

Jean T. Strandness

Like many consortia nationally in the late 1960s and early 1970s, the Tri-College University (TCU) consortium formed, in large part, to facilitate cross-registration opportunities and joint academic programs for students of its member institutions. A North Dakota nonprofit corporation licensed to do business in Minnesota, TCU is a consortium of three institutions of higher education in the metropolitan twin cities of Moorhead, Minnesota, and Fargo, North Dakota: Concordia College, a liberal arts, church-affiliated private college, with an enrollment of three thousand students; Moorhead State University (MSU), a public undergraduate and graduate university, with an enrollment of sixty-five hundred students; and North Dakota State University (NDSU), a public, land-grant research university, with an enrollment of more than ninety-five hundred students.

Implementing Cross-Registration

Since the formal incorporation of the TCU consortium in 1970, thirty-three thousand students have taken more than ninety-five thousand courses through cross-registration. A number of initial and ongoing principles have contributed to the success of this consortial enterprise, which form the basis for the suggestions that follow.

Carefully assess the complementariness of the course offerings of the institutions entering into a consortial agreement. Member institutions should each possess varying curricular strengths that are mutually beneficial. Institutions of higher education too similar or too different in nature are not likely to be suitable partners.

Consider what effects distance among member institutions might have on cross-registration. Although located in different states, the TCU member institutions are close together. Concordia College and MSU are within walking distance of each other, and the distance from North Dakota State University to the other two institutions is just over four miles. Many students drive to classes on the other campuses, and public transportation is available. Although rapidly increasing distance education capabilities certainly call for a redefinition of such terms as *proximity,* actual physical proximity is helpful.

Seek the approval of all necessary governing bodies. All boards of trustees and state boards of higher education should endorse the cross-registration initiative. Because the Tri-College University consortium crosses state boundaries, special legislation was passed in Minnesota and North Dakota at the time of its inception in the late 1960s.

Allow each member institution to determine its own procedures. Currently, in the TCU consortium, no limits are placed on the number of courses MSU students may take at NDSU, and vice versa. As a private institution, Concordia College has determined that Concordia students—and MSU or NDSU students wishing to do course work at Concordia—may take only one course per semester through cross-registration, and then only if they are full-time students and if that course is not available on their home campus. Even though all three member institutions are fully committed to consortial cross-registration, campus cultures call for somewhat different regulations. Allowing for such differences ensures that consortial cooperation will continue in a collegial way.

Make cross-registration procedures clear and easy. Each TCU member institution has its own specially designated registrar to assist with all cross-registration courses. Students register on their home campus and pay home-campus tuition. At the end of the semester, the course grade appears on the home-campus transcript.

Encourage registrars of the member institutions to communicate regularly. Both formally, in meetings, and informally, via phone and e-mail, the registrars of the TCU institutions discuss current issues. Recently, for example, the registrars have begun discussing how Tri-College registration might be facilitated using newly available electronic registration systems.

Strive to achieve complementary campus calendars. Currently, the calendars of the TCU member institutions are closely aligned. From 1992 to 1995, however, complementary campus calendars were not possible because NDSU shifted from quarters to semesters in 1992, while MSU remained on a quarter system. During this three-year period, enrollment through cross-registration decreased, due at least in part to the differences in campus calendars. Consequently, Moorhead State University took the initiative within the Minnesota State University System to shift its calendar to semesters. By the beginning of Fall 1995, all three institutions were on a semester system and starting classes within a week of one another. Since then, course enrollments through cross-registration have increased every year.

Arrange for convenient transportation among campuses. The TCU consortium works with the Fargo-Moorhead Metro Area Transit office to ensure that students are able to travel from campus to campus by bus on a travel schedule that is aligned with class schedules. The Moorhead and Fargo bus services are very efficient, running among the campuses every half hour from early morning to early evening. Some consortia provide their own intercampus transportation, sometimes at no cost to students.

Provide free parking for students from other campuses. TCU students who have a home-campus parking permit can park free in designated lots on the other two campuses.

Educate students and faculty about cross-registration possibilities on an ongoing basis through a variety of means. At the beginning of each fall semester, the consortium office creates an annual student guide to consortium programs and services, which is distributed to all academic advisers and students, and is also available in all three registrars' offices and the consortium office throughout the year. This information is also posted on a web site [www.ndsu.nodak.edu/tricollege], which is linked to the home pages of the member institutions. In addition, specially designed posters promoting cross-registration and other TCU services appear on bulletin boards on all three campuses. Having information readily available is important, considering that even veteran faculty advisers may not be completely familiar with cross-registration procedures and that each student who goes through the process for the first time is likely to have questions. Also, given that new faculty join each campus annually and every year brings new freshmen classes, it is important to find mechanisms to inform each new group about cross-registration—for example, through presentations at orientation sessions for new faculty and students.

Sustain a stable "balance of trade" through regular collegial communication. The TCU provost and the vice presidents for academic affairs of the three member institutions (the TCU commissioners) collectively review the cross-registration enrollment figures on an annual basis to ensure that the balance of trade remains relatively even. If traffic were to begin to flow too heavily in one direction, an institution might place limitations on the number of courses that its students could take through cross-registration for a period of time.

Decide whether or not to develop a payment formula to redress excessive exchange imbalances, should they occur. Although the TCU consortium has not needed to apply its payment formula for many years, the formula exists, should the need occur. Essentially, no reimbursement is expected until the annual credit-hour imbalance exceeds one faculty FTE. Then, should an imbalance occur, the dollar equivalent for an FTE would be calculated using the minimum figure for employing a faculty member at the institution receiving payment. The nature of such a formula, of course, varies from consortium to consortium. Furthermore, some consortia have chosen to have no payment formula at all. These consortia operate under the principle that, because cross-registration is possible only as long as seats in a class are available, no real costs are incurred and therefore no monies need be exchanged, even when excessive exchange imbalances occur. Regardless of the collective decision, a consortium is well advised to consider in advance whether a payment formula for excessive exchange imbalances should exist and, if so, what its nature should be.

Benefits of Cross-Registration

Directly or indirectly, cross-registration benefits its member institutions in several ways. For example, cross-registration increases educational opportunities for students of member institutions. Students may enrich their course of study by taking one or several special-interest elective courses that are available on another campus but not on their home campus. Also, students may earn a minor (and possibly a second major) from another institution, thereby complementing their home-campus major. Under a TCU "covered-program" consortial agreement, students who wish to remain at their home institution as long as possible (perhaps for financial-aid reasons) can begin taking courses toward a major at another institution during their sophomore and junior years through cross-registration and wait to transfer to that institution, from which they ultimately will receive their degree, until their senior year. Currently, two joint majors exist through the TCU consortium—a graduate program in Educational Leadership and an undergraduate Nursing program—both of which use TCU cross-registration.

Another benefit is that cross-registration is a powerful recruiting tool. Admissions officers report that being able to take courses at all three schools with no cost beyond the home-campus tuition is very appealing to prospective students, even if they never take advantage of cross-registration possibilities.

And finally, cross-registration generates cost savings for member institutions. Course offerings on other campuses amplify each institution's curriculum, providing students with more diverse possibilities than any one institution could conceivably make available alone. If Chinese language courses are offered at Moorhead State University, Concordia College and North Dakota State University can reasonably assume that Chinese is a program they do not need to develop. In making decisions about faculty hires and program development, the three academic vice presidents and the two state boards of higher education will consider existing resources in other institutions in the TCU consortium, carefully deliberating about curriculum expansion in areas already available in another institution within the consortium.

Establishing Joint Academic Programs

Two joint academic programs exist in the TCU consortium: a graduate program in Educational Leadership, founded in 1974, with MSU and NDSU as the partnering institutions, and an undergraduate Nursing program, founded in 1982, with Concordia College and NDSU as the partnering institutions. Both programs developed to respond to identified regional needs that no single institution within the consortial group could address alone. Both programs were planned and are maintained by the participating institutions. Both are accredited. The students of each joint program graduate from the institution in which they are enrolled.

The faculty of the graduate Educational Leadership (formerly Educational Administration) program have opted to rotate the chair's position so that it alternates between the MSU and NDSU faculties on a three-year basis. The program faculty engage in a certain amount of distance education and practicum field work and have even become involved in joint program collaboration with other institutions in the Minnesota and North Dakota university systems. Approximately four hundred students have completed master's and specialist's degrees since the joint program was formed.

By contrast, the chair of the Nursing program was appointed to that role in 1984 and has continued to chair the program since then. Nursing admits twenty-five students per campus each year to its upper-level program. Students generally take their junior-level courses at Concordia College and their senior-level courses at NDSU. Recently, the department has been experimenting with faculty exchanges so that students can spend more time on their home campus during their senior year.

Benefits of Joint Academic Programs

Both department heads, Dennis Van Berkum, chair of Educational Leadership, and Lois Nelson, chair of Nursing, see a number of positive outcomes resulting from the kind of joint program they chair:

A program that cannot be created by one campus alone can be formed by pooling faculty resources from two campuses.

A combined faculty produces a stronger, more diverse curriculum.

Participating institutions tend not to duplicate faculty expertise, so the program can be broader. Faculty can teach courses more often and still sustain research in their areas of specialization.

Institutions share costs. Each hires half the faculty and splits the costs of operation, accreditation, and professional memberships.

Granting agencies and accrediting bodies, though they may have some initial questions, are inclined to regard cooperative joint programs very favorably.

The paradigm of cooperation generates a creative mind-set in which faculty are likely to develop a strong esprit de corps and maintain an affirmative attitude so that, when problems arise in the cooperative venture, they seek proactive solutions.

In general, the shared sense that cooperation is a positive good increases faculty morale and productivity.

Some Important Considerations

Although the benefits achieved through joint academic programs are many, the challenges involved can be considerable as well, and certain cautions are necessary:

Starting a new program on an interinstitutional cooperative basis is much more likely to be successful than an effort to merge two existing departments on different campuses.

Establishing a joint program requires extensive planning, and all necessary campus governance bodies and institutional boards of control must approve the program.

Achieving consensus and sustaining trust among all the necessary parties in two (or more) institutions requires energy, vigilant communication, patience, and diplomacy on the part of the program chair.

Sustaining support for a joint academic program is an ongoing process. Whenever key decision makers on any of the campuses change, a process of reeducation regarding the nature of the joint program must take place.

Obtaining support may be difficult. Some faculty and administrators may be reluctant to commit fully to a cooperative program, which takes extra time to maintain and may be viewed as a fiscal competitor with an institution's internal programs.

Running a joint program takes additional time and energy, and the program chair must be willing to take on a heavy load.

Because of the complexities involved in administering a joint program, the program chair must be a skilled manager, a good communicator, and an adept diplomat. Fortunately, those occupying such a position are generally highly committed to the long-term sustenance of the program, often having been involved in its creation.

Other Kinds of Consortial Academic Cooperation

Although cross-registration and joint academic programs are the primary modes of consortial academic cooperation, a number of other opportunities exist as well.

Collaborative Scheduling. Established programs in member institutions that are experiencing reduced enrollment of majors can benefit from collaborative scheduling in conjunction with cross-registration, which allows upper-level, specialized courses to be taught more regularly and to a larger group of students at one time. Programs within the TCU consortium that have engaged in collaborative scheduling are Business Administration, Economics, Mathematics, and Physics. Faculty are generally supportive of such an endeavor, which increases educational opportunities for their students.

Joint Faculty Appointments. When no single member institution wants to establish a full-time position in a specialized area, and two or more participating members are interested in committing to a portion of a full-time position, a joint appointment through the consortium is worth considering. Currently, the TCU consortium members share the salary costs for a tenure-track percussionist position. This assistant professor teaches on all three campuses and coordinates and conducts the Tri-College Percussion Ensemble and Marimba Choir, made up of students from all three institutions. Certain modern languages and other specialized academic disciplines might also be candidates for a joint faculty appointment.

Team-Taught Seminars. In the early 1970s, the Tri-College University consortium received major funding from the National Endowment for the Humanities and the Bremer Foundation to establish an interdisciplinary seminar in the humanities, team-taught by three faculty members, one from each campus. Former students and faculty still talk about how stimulating this academic experience was for all who participated.

Since 1989, an interinstitutional World Studies faculty committee has organized a multidisciplinary course each semester, which rotates from campus to campus. These World Studies Seminars have focused either on a world region or single country—so far including Latin America, East Asia, Africa, the Middle East, China, India, Brazil, and Mexico—or on a significant global topic—so far including communications, ethics, women's issues, terrorism, the North American Free Trade Agreement, the U.N. Universal Declaration of Human Rights, and nutrition, health, and the environment. One faculty member serves as principal coordinator, drawing on faculty expertise from all three campuses for individual lectures, for which invited faculty are paid a modest honorarium. Here too, both students and faculty appreciate the intellectual stimulation and collegiality that this consortial joint venture provides.

Colloquia and Lectureships. The three physics departments sponsor Tri-College seminars for physics majors and faculty. The three mathematics departments offer a series of mathematics colloquia, open to all students and faculty, which rotate among the campuses. The three history departments sponsor an annual Tri-College History Lecture, which rotates among the institutions and is delivered each year by a selected faculty member. These and other cooperative events sustain a sense of intellectual community within the consortium.

Research and Outreach Centers. The TCU consortium serves as a nexus for faculty from the three campuses who wish to collaborate on research projects and to seek external funding on a joint basis. Long-term collaborations sometimes coalesce into formal cooperative centers—for example, the Center for Economic Education, the Center for Environmental Studies, the Center for Third World Studies, and the Regional International Trade Association. The consortium can be very useful in facilitating the organization of such academic research and outreach centers and can serve as the fiscal agent for funded projects.

Conclusion

Institutions of higher education can cooperate consortially through collaborative academic ventures, even as they continue to compete as individual institutions. Cross-registration and joint programs provide member institutions of consortia with opportunities to conserve fiscal resources while increasing educational opportunities for students and enhancing collegial interaction among faculty.

JEAN T. STRANDNESS is provost of the Tri-College University consortium in Moorhead, Minnesota and Fargo, North Dakota.

Collaborative admissions and recruitment in colleges and universities are possible, even among institutions that compete for students.

Collaborative Admissions and Recruitment Practices

Barbara Bradley Stonewater

When someone connected with higher education thinks about interinstitutional collaboration, admissions and recruitment are not the first areas that come to mind. Historically, even in periods when potential college students were plentiful, colleges and universities, particularly those of the same type or those in close geographic proximity, have been competitive. Indeed, even in consortia or other collaborative arrangements where cooperation is the norm in many other areas, admissions and recruitment are difficult areas in which to rise above the natural tendency toward competition.

In the Greater Cincinnati Consortium of Colleges and Universities (GCCCU), which has an almost thirty-year history of collaboration and cooperation at many levels and in a wide range of areas, developing a true cooperative spirit among admissions officers has at times been difficult. However, a cooperative culture is slowly being developed, which ultimately will benefit all institutions and their potential students. This chapter will describe practices, programs, and ideas for institutions to work together in the recruitment of students. Many of these programs have been tried and are successful, in GCCCU and elsewhere, whereas others are still under development. Clearly, various consortia and other cooperative arrangements have different needs and possibilities for such cooperation, but I hope that some of the programs described here will be useful to other collaborative groups.

Underlying Philosophy

Simply because a group of colleges and universities is organized into a formal consortial arrangement does not automatically lead to successful cooperation in the recruitment and admission of students. The three key ingredients for success are (1) a commitment from the presidents and key admissions personnel, (2) consistent work and contact among staff, both within the institutions and the consortium office, and (3) a belief in the benefit of collaboration to all institutions and to the communities they serve.

Commitment. Typically when a consortium is formed, the chief executive officers formalize a commitment to work together for a wide variety of reasons. For institutions to work together successfully in admissions, this commitment needs to be clearly made and articulated at the top, not only by the presidents but by the administrators responsible for the recruitment and admissions process. If an institution is not committed at both levels and makes decisions based solely on its own interests, the benefits gained from working together in the admissions arena are not likely to be realized. Staff at all levels must get the consistent message that, though their own institution is the top priority, it is also important to work in the best interest of potential students and the larger arena in which their institution is located.

Consistent Contact. A second ingredient in true cooperation in an area like admissions is a sense of trust among those working together. Trust means knowing that all institutions are playing by the same rules and will not take undue advantage of the others. That trust can be developed through ongoing relationships among admissions staff and the chief admissions or recruitment officer. Within GCCCU, the admissions staff has worked together over the years at the National College Fair held in Cincinnati through joint trips, projects, and publications. The chief enrollment officers meet regularly to share common concerns and, in the process, have developed a sense of trust and comfort with each other and the other institutions. Consequently, those involved know that all come to the table with appropriate collaborative goals while still recognizing and understanding their competition with each other.

Belief in Benefit to All. This is probably the most important condition and perhaps the most difficult to achieve. If presidents and chief enrollment officers within a collaborative group of institutions believe that finding and attracting qualified students is a zero sum game in which one institution gains only at another's expense, true collaboration is difficult. However, if those involved believe that the pool of qualified applicants is indeed expandable and that they can reach some potential students collaboratively in ways they cannot individually, then a true cooperative spirit can develop. Each institution must continue to pursue aggressively its own recruitment goals while understanding that some of those goals can be attained under a cooperative banner. Developing this belief depends to some extent on commitment and trust.

Collaborative Projects

It is within the context of these underlying conditions that real collaboration in admissions and recruitment can flourish among institutions. The ideas for such collaboration suggested here are in the areas of (1) written materials, (2) recruitment events, (3) presentations, (4) joint trips or visits, and (5) the use of electronic media.

Written Materials. This is perhaps one of the easiest areas in which to gain cooperation, as it often has clear financial savings for member institutions, but it is often overlooked.

Joint brochures and posters, which list simply the most basic information about the cooperating institutions, can be very effective when distributed to area high schools, libraries, churches, community centers, vocational schools, and other locations. The Colleges of Worcester Consortium in Worcester, Massachusetts, and the Colleges of the Fenway in the Boston area are but two of the many consortia that facilitate such joint publications. Often these are eye-catching publications that simply list the member institutions and their admissions contact information. The advantage is that a potential student can see what institutions exist in the location of interest and obtain the essential information easily and quickly.

The next level of joint publications is represented by two projects of GCCCU, one that was completed two years ago and one that is under development. The first was the publication of the *Guide to Higher Education in Greater Cincinnati*—a booklet containing consistent facts about each institution, a brief description of each, and a matrix at the back listing degree programs cross-referenced by institution. Although many found this helpful, and it was the first time such information had been available in one place, it may have been too much information in a too-long format. On review, GCCCU decided not to reprint it in the same format. Consequently, the project under development currently is a brochure containing essential admissions and financial aid information about those institutions in GCCCU offering undergraduate programs. This brochure will contain contact information (telephone number, e-mail address, and web site), as well as special deadlines, required tests, scholarships, and so forth. This information will be combined with a basic checklist of tasks that high school students should be engaged in, from middle school through their senior year, to prepare for college. The goal of this publication is to provide, in one place, all the basics that a student needs to complete an application to one or more colleges in greater Cincinnati. The plan is to use various forms of this information for shorter flyers, posters, and activities for each grade level, using the same language and information.

Although clearly, there is a financial cost to such joint publications, such information can be used in ways that individual recruitment information cannot, and joint expenditures may result in cost savings.

Recruitment Events. A number of higher education consortia across the country have sponsored various types of mini-college fairs, often under the sponsorship of high schools, churches, or community centers. One of the pitfalls of events sponsored by outside organizations is that often only certain institutions are invited because the organization is not aware of all the colleges and universities or does not have appropriate contacts. Consequently, potential students may not get a complete picture of educational opportunities.

When institutions are truly working cooperatively with the intention that all institutions be included and broad-based information provided, the information provided is more comprehensive. Even though only staff from certain institutions may be present, they will provide information about all institutions, not just their own. In that kind of context, the information provided is perceived as being more complete, objective, and disseminated in the best interest of the students.

One example of this within GCCCU is at the graduate level. After various piecemeal efforts at recruiting graduate students locally, the eleven institutions within GCCCU with graduate programs joined forces for a Graduate Recruitment Fair, with the result of attracting more people than any institution had ever been able to individually. There have been similar successes at the undergraduate level, both within GCCCU and other consortia.

Collaborative Presentations. The typical model for admissions, recruitment, and financial aid presentations for colleges and universities at high schools and other organizations is similar to that of consortial mini-fairs. A high school asks admissions or financial aid representatives from one or more institutions to give information on some aspect of the admissions process, sometimes with the expectation that the representatives will provide information about their own institution and furnish broader information as well. GCCCU has discovered, however, in extensive conversations with high school personnel and other community organizations, that even though the information provided goes beyond the represented college or university, the person delivering the message is seen only as a representative of that institution, with all the inherent biases. Consequently, GCCCU is in the process of developing interinstitutional presentation teams. These would be groups of two or three admissions or financial aid staff members representing different institutions, who would go out under the consortium umbrella to give presentations in areas such as choosing the right college, negotiating the ACT and SAT, filling out college applications, writing the admissions essay, finding scholarships and other sources of financial aid, or some combination of these topics. When the team comes as GCCCU representatives and presents broad-based information, which certainly may also include specifics on a given college, the information is perceived as unbiased and more credible. In addition, such teams have access to groups and organizations that would not be interested in a hard-sell presentation on an individual institution. The downside of such presentations is that institutions make decisions about their level of participation based in large part on the benefit to them. Thus, different institutional goals, size of staff, and other variables may result in less than complete collaboration.

This type of project requires some education and training of institutional staffs and the kind of commitment indicated earlier. Team members must truly believe that these kinds of interinstitutional presentations are, in fact, in the best interest of potential students, the individual institutions, and higher education as a broader entity. An additional advantage of such efforts is that the presentations do not require additional financial commitments on the part of the consortium or the colleges and universities.

Joint Trips or Visits. Another area for possible and often successful collaboration is the joint sponsorship of visits by high school counselors to member colleges and universities, as well as joint trips by admissions personnel to high schools and other organizations.

For a number of years, GCCCU sponsored visits by groups of high school counselors and arranged for these counselors to visit all of the area institutions during one trip. Often this involved planning transportation, campus tours, meetings with individual admissions and financial aid staffs, meals, conversations with current students, and other events designed to acquaint counselors with area institutions. Such counselor tours are common in a number of consortia and represent a good way to pool funds and effort and attract counselors who might not otherwise have the opportunity to visit all of the campuses.

A somewhat reverse strategy is to have admissions or financial aid personnel visit high schools in groups, somewhat like the mini-fairs described earlier. This could be done within the local region but could also be effective in neighboring cities or regions. Although all colleges and universities have certain high schools and regions that they visit on a regular basis, collaborating on such trips may give an institution access to a high school or group of schools that they would not have on their own. This is different from the collaborative presentation mentioned earlier in that, in these joint trips, the institutional representatives are, in fact, recruiting for their own institution but doing it more efficiently by traveling with others. Although this kind of cooperation does not require the same kind of reeducation that the collaborative, consortial presentations do, there is still a level of commitment to working together for the good of all potential students that is necessary for success.

Electronic Media. The rapid and ever-changing development of the World Wide Web and the electronic media has opened up new possibilities for information dissemination and will continue to do so as more developments occur. Although the immediate and obvious effect is for individual institutions to make increasing information available on the Web and through their web site, including electronic submission of application materials, there are also increasing possibilities for collaboration.

Within GCCCU, a major goal for the consortium web site is to be the starting point for any and all information about higher education in the greater Cincinnati area. This may include academic program information, course schedules, consortium programs such as cross-registration, and other types of information. However, one of the most effective uses of the web site seems to be to have all the admissions and financial aid information available from one starting point. This can be done with simple links from the consortium web site to the individual institution's home pages, admissions, or financial aid pages; the links are fairly simple to establish.

Another level would be to have an interactive capability that would enable the prospective student to do a search for a college along certain variables. These are currently available nationally, but sometimes students who for various reasons want to restrict their search to a local area could benefit from such an opportunity on a more manageable and localized basis. Other ideas could be developed to enable prospective students to find information, explore institutions, and submit applications from one electronic point. The benefit is, as in other ideas described here, for potential students to be able to find the information they need easily. Although development of a consortium web site that provides such access to information may involve some financial commitment by the consortium or its individual institutions, the cost may be minimal for the additional exposure and benefit to each.

Conclusion

Even though all the projects and ideas described in this chapter may not be appropriate for a particular cooperative group of institutions, some are likely to be. At least they will stimulate additional thinking about using existing talent, contacts, experience, and budgets to combine efforts, minimize duplication, and provide better and more complete information about the opportunities at a group of institutions. As state funds and private resources become less plentiful and the public served by higher education makes increasing demands, it is becoming clear that each college and university cannot be all things to all people. As we seek to focus our institutions on our own "pockets of excellence" and at the same time provide all that our regions demand and deserve, cooperation and collaboration may well become a key ingredient in the survival of all in the kind of postsecondary education climate that will meet the public needs and continue to foster economic and educational development.

BARBARA BRADLEY STONEWATER is executive director of the Greater Cincinnati Consortium of Colleges and Universities in Cincinnati, Ohio.

The success of the Summer Institute on College Teaching shows how consortia can fill the needs of member institutions for faculty development programs.

Faculty Development: Working Together to Improve Teaching and Learning

Lawrence G. Dotolo

The Virginia Tidewater Consortium for Higher Education has been involved in faculty development for the past twenty years. What started as a chance involvement has turned out to be a highly developed and well-organized program that serves hundreds of faculty from Consortium institutions.

Twenty years ago, the Kansas City Regional Council for Higher Education invited the Virginia Tidewater Consortium to participate in a faculty development program funded by the Kellogg Foundation. The project required that each participating consortium send an administrator and a faculty member to a dissemination conference to determine the best way for consortia to become involved in developing faculty development programs. Each consortium present was to develop its own plan to fit the individual requirements of its colleges and universities. The Virginia Tidewater Consortium's plan was simple: establish a summer program that would deal with basic pedagogy and improve teaching at the college level. The W. K. Kellogg Foundation, through the Kansas City Regional Council for Higher Education, provided $15,000 to each consortium to develop its own strategies for implementing a faculty development program. The Virginia Tidewater Consortium used the grant to develop its program, which came to be known as the Summer Institute on College Teaching.

The Kansas City Regional Council's Kellogg Foundation effort, as presented to the other consortia, was for the most part an administrative exercise. The Virginia Tidewater Consortium had no idea how the faculty would respond or what improvements faculty actually needed. Thus the consortium established a faculty development committee, with a faculty representative from each participating institution. After a month of discussion and planning, the consortium developed the specifics of the Summer Institute on College Teaching. The consortium advertised the program among the institutions and was surprised that the response was so great. Limited to twenty-five faculty, the consortium's program was quickly oversubscribed. The large number of responses required that the consortium limit the number of faculty per institution. What the consortium learned from the experience was that there was indeed a demand by the faculty for programs dealing with the various aspects of college teaching and learning.

Reasons a Consortial Setting Made Sense

Although the consortium realized that the interest in faculty development was widespread, its only offering was the Summer Institute on College Teaching. Most of the colleges and universities within the consortium had no formal faculty development program, and most administrators thought that sending faculty to conferences was sufficient faculty development. However, once the administrations began to require faculty to be evaluated by students, and once department chairs and division chairs began to keep records of the student evaluations, everyone involved realized that a more organized, systematic approach to improving teaching and learning was required.

None of the colleges had faculty development programs; furthermore, most faculty were not sure that they wanted to be involved in programs designed and promoted by their own institution. The consortium became a clear alternative. It was so because the consortium

- Was the only higher education organization with the experience and expertise needed to run a credible and well-defined program
- Sponsored an institute—the Summer Institute on College Teaching—with an excellent reputation
- Had developed a clear idea about the programs needed
- Could provide the leadership needed to design and implement a consistent faculty development program
- Could provide quality programs because the institutions shared the expenses for offering the seminar and workshops

The consortium decided to expand its faculty development from the summer institute to a program that took place during the academic year. Therefore, the consortium began to offer workshops and seminars on enhancing college teaching and learning that would be available to faculty during the academic year and would provide them with skills they could use immediately in their classrooms. The practical, hands-on nature of the programs was very attractive to faculty.

Search for Outside Funding

Because of the great demand for programs designed for enhancing teaching and learning at the college level, the Virginia Tidewater Consortium for Higher Education sought outside funding to develop a full-time, consortiumwide faculty development program. After some disappointments in finding a funding agency, the consortium eventually obtained funding from the Pew Charitable Trusts for two years. The $150,000 grant enabled the consortium to develop its own Center for Teaching Effectiveness. But more important, it gave the consortium the ability to create faculty development programs throughout the year using the best people in higher education who were involved in enhancing teaching and learning.

In addition, many faculty liked the consortium arrangement because it gave them the opportunity to meet faculty from other colleges and to interact with people from different academic areas.

The Consortium's Program

Almost all of the faculty programs are held on Saturdays and, without exception, the attendance is always high, even though faculty give up a full day of their weekend to participate in a teaching workshop and have not asked for, nor do they receive, a stipend. The faculty express appreciation for the consortium's effort, and it is clear that the majority want to improve their teaching and want to learn more about teaching and learning. Many of the consultants have commented on the dedication of the individuals and are amazed at the numbers of faculty who attend. The consortium offers the faculty members a continental breakfast and lunch for a nominal fee; there is no charge for the seminar or workshop.

Another important factor is that the majority of the faculty who attend consortium programs have had little or no training in the basics of teaching. For example, it is common that faculty who have never had a course in testing still base their entire grading system on tests that are, for the most part, full of test errors and consequently invalid.

The consortium program thus fills a real need—a need that is not being met by any of the colleges and universities. In fact, one college president of one of the member institutions of the Virginia Tidewater Consortium stated that he would rather give his faculty development money to the consortium because of the high quality of its programs and because his faculty did not feel that the administration was singling them out.

Because the consortium faculty development programs have been so successful and the colleges and universities have come to look for programs designed by the consortium, there was little doubt that the colleges and universities would want the program to continue beyond the grant cycle. Thus the consortium's program became an important part of what the colleges continue to offer their faculty for the enhancement of teaching and learning.

The Virginia Tidewater Consortium offers a fall faculty development program that deals with essentially the same topics each year: testing, lecturing, and questioning skills. The program is held Friday afternoon and all day Saturday and is designed for all faculty, regardless of teaching experience. Most of the colleges require that all newly hired faculty attend the program and, in most cases, it is the only pedagogy-related program that newly hired faculty have an opportunity to attend. The commitment by the institutions to faculty development programs makes it easier for the faculty from various institutions within the consortium to participate, and the consortium has established an attractive atmosphere for faculty looking for programs. Faculty, for the most part, like the interinstitutional aspect of the programs, and many have established working relationships with faculty from other schools from the same or related academic areas. They soon come to realize that their concerns are universal and that faculty from very different types of institutions have very similar concerns—student attendance, student preparedness, student evaluations, and their own classroom presentations.

One of the great strengths of the Virginia Tidewater Consortium's faculty development program is the diversity of the faculty that participate and the institutions they represent. Faculty come from all disciplines and all types of institutions (community colleges, liberal arts institutions, universities, a medical school, a graduate-only institution, a military-graduate school, and two predominantly black institutions). The bond that brings them together is the desire to improve their teaching and to learn more about how their students learn. The consortium provides the mechanism for them to meet to discuss teaching and learning.

Elements of a Successful Program

A consortium, or any formal alliance of colleges, can be the vehicle through which college and university faculties can work together to enhance the atmosphere of teaching and learning on their campuses. The following elements are needed so that schools can be effective in working together in improving teaching and learning:

- The colleges and universities must be close enough together that faculty can drive to them in two hours at the maximum.
- Someone has to devote time and energy to take the lead in calling meetings and sending out notices of the workshops and seminars to faculty.
- Faculty representatives from each college and university must be willing to serve on a consortium faculty development committee to determine the programs to be offered.
- The institutions involved in the cooperative effort must be willing to share the expenses of consultants, materials, luncheons, and so on, for the programs.
- The institutions involved must endorse teaching as an important endeavor on their own campuses.

- The institutions must be willing to encourage faculty to attend consortium faculty development programs.
- Administrators should attend these faculty seminars to learn more about the issues of teaching and learning that concern faculty.

Although programs can be successful if some of the elements listed are missing, the Virginia Tidewater Consortium's experience has been that a great majority must be operating for the programs to continue long term. Faculty development requires commitment and dedication if it is to be sustained. Almost any institution or group of institutions can be successful in presenting one or two seminars; however, long-term success requires organization, dedication, and the ability to determine faculty needs.

Another important aspect for a successful program is support from the top. When, at a consortium board meeting, the college presidents agree that a consortium faculty development program is important, the program is more likely to work. Academic administrators, department or division chairs, deans, and provosts will follow the lead of the presidents. This support makes it easier for the consortium faculty development committee to work, and it makes the coordinating work of the consortium central office easier and more effective. Also, once the consortium faculty development is established, continued support from academic administrators is of great benefit.

Even with full support from presidents and academic administrators, a consortium must continually advertise its programs. The Virginia Tidewater Consortium does this by creating flyers for each of its seminars or workshops and mailing them to the faculty at each institution. Consortium faculty-development committee members are responsible for encouraging participation by their faculty. In addition, the consortium places information about the programs on its web site and has recently established a listserve for faculty from its institutions.

Why Consortia Should Be Involved

Faculty development is one of the most important programs in which consortia can be involved. As institutions come under closer scrutiny by state agencies and boards of visitors because of their greater-than-inflation tuition increases, they have to show that they are concerned with trying to improve the teaching effectiveness of their faculties. Too many complaints by students, parents, and alumni about the quality of teaching have found their way to state legislators and boards of visitors, and these can be extremely detrimental to any institution of higher education. Institutions need to respond by indicating that teaching is important and that there is a mechanism whereby colleges and universities are striving to enhance teaching and learning. Colleges and universities working together in a consortial setting makes perfect sense because it sets the tone for all colleges in the area. It sends a strong message to legislators and boards of visitors from the academic community that those in higher education value teaching and learning.

Almost any consortium can undertake faculty development if it has the desire and perseverance. It not only takes the sharing of resources but also the sharing of a collective vision. It requires that institutions give up some autonomy for the larger, more important issue: improved teaching and learning. Although some national organizations attempt to involve colleges and universities in the faculty development issue, they cannot do so as effectively because they are remote from the campuses and the faculty. Consortium programs establish a sense of community among faculty. Regardless of background, institution, gender, nationality, age, and race, they establish bonds based on a concern for teaching and learning. Consortium programs attract full- and part-time faculty, and in the workshops and seminars there are no second-class citizens. Part-time faculty often do not attend departmental or division meetings, but they do attend consortium programs because they know there is no pressure, no scrutiny, and no prejudice. For them, as for most of the participants, teaching and learning are the most important aspects of academic life.

Most faculty realize that, unlike their colleagues in elementary and secondary education, they have not been trained in pedagogy. College-level teaching becomes on-the-job training, and most institutions are not prepared, nor do they have the resources to offer some kind of remediation. Consortial programs are one way that colleges and universities can afford to meet the need. It is extremely difficult for individual institutions to sustain a faculty development program; institutions working together make the faculty development more cost-effective and more efficient.

The importance of faculty development programs to consortia should not be underestimated, nor should the work needed to keep them going. Although the traditional modes of cooperation for consortia such as cross-registration, library cooperation, and cooperative degree programs are quite easily managed once established, a consortiumwide faculty development program requires a continuously proactive position. The consortium involved in improving teaching and learning must be prepared to devote staff time and resources to its programs.

An effective faculty development program does not need to offer a multitude of workshops and seminars. The Virginia Tidewater Consortium learned that faculty time is important, that asking faculty to give up more than three to four weekends per semester is a lot. If faculty feel that there are too many programs, they may become immune to the notices and the programs will not be well attended.

Conclusion

Faculty development in a consortial setting is a project in which most consortia can be involved if their schools are within reasonable proximity. It is the kind of project that brings faculty from various institutions together, and it creates an atmosphere whereby teaching and learning become more highly valued. Offering faculty an opportunity to meet and to discuss teaching and learning issues is important; doing it in a consortial setting is efficient and has a greater impact. In the last analysis, a consortiumwide faculty development program is a project that can have an important and positive effect on the institutions involved, their faculty, and their students.

LAWRENCE G. DOTOLO *is president of the Virginia Tidewater Consortium for Higher Education and executive director of the Association for Consortium Leadership.*

Cooperative fundraising has become an essential item on any consortium's agenda, even though it is difficult to ask institutions to raise funds in consort.

Consortial Fundraising

Lorna M. Peterson

Five Colleges, Inc., whose members are Amherst, Hampshire, Mount Holyoke, Smith, and the University of Massachusetts, Amherst, is one of few established consortia of higher education with a development officer on staff. We have had one since 1982. Development, or fundraising, is limited in our case to grants and contracts—mostly grants—from both government agencies and private foundations. Solicitation of individual donors is not sanctioned, although there have been one or two exceptions.

In the last decade, grant funds have constituted between 25 and 35 percent of the Five College annual budget of approximately $4.5 million. Even before Five Colleges was incorporated, its member institutions had jointly applied for and received grants to promote collaboration and draw the institutions closer together. As far back as 1955, the work of a "committee on cooperation" that was charged with exploring ways colleges could share resources was supported by a grant from the Fund for the Advancement of Education. Other grants followed in increasing numbers once the consortium was established in 1965; a full-time staff was appointed in 1967, and cooperative programs were expanded. Along with the expansion came a greater need for external support. Support came in the form of planning and implementation grants.

In the early years and throughout the 1970s, no established policy existed for seeking outside funding. Some ground rules did exist, however. The coordinator (the chief executive officer of Five Colleges) could not act independently of the institutions. Any grant proposal, or even a letter of inquiry, had to be approved by all the institutions. One of the first memos I remember reading when I joined the Five College staff in 1980 was a memo to the five directors of development detailing a process for obtaining approval. Essentially, the

policy required the coordinator to disseminate among the development officers a list of all the foundations being considered for a consortial approach.
Each development officer could then eliminate any of the foundations listed if
there was a conflict—real or perceived—with institutional plans "in the fore-
seeable future." As can easily be imagined, by the time the list made its rounds
to each campus and was returned to the Five College office, there were few, if
any, foundation names remaining. Clearly, this procedure was not promising.
It did, however, highlight a major issue: potential competition with and among
the member institutions.

Another issue we addressed early on was that of credibility. Funding agencies, whether private or governmental, are often suspicious of consortia. They
question the long-term commitment both to the consortium itself and to the
particular project. They ask, "Is it important to the institutions or is it marginal?" They wonder about the support that consortial proposals have from
each individual campus and the ability of the consortium to implement the
grant if awarded. Frequently they are also worried about whether the partnership will survive the grant period. In other words, consortia, especially new
ones, often do not have a strong enough track record.

A third concern is that of grant administration. Who will be the fiscal
agent? Who will provide oversight for the grant? In the case of consortia like
Five Colleges, Inc., which has its own business office and treasurer, there is
usually no problem, although stewardship is always an issue when the principal investigator or the project director(s) are on another campus. If an independent business or grants office does not exist, responsibility for fiscal as well
as program management must be negotiated among the member institutions.

The climate of the nineties has forced higher education to look carefully
at its financing. The pressure to reduce costs, to eliminate redundancies, to
stop raising tuition is constant. Under these conditions, funding agencies and
the institutions themselves have come to realize the benefits of a collaborative
approach. Foundations and governmental agencies are directly encouraging
institutions to work together and issuing requests for proposals (RFP) to
encourage partnerships. Currently, when cooperative programs and joint ventures are being so strongly promoted, it is extremely important for consortia
to develop fundraising guidelines and to have in place a policy that supports
those efforts. Any policy that is developed will have to address the three issues
noted: competition, credibility, and stewardship.

The policy currently in place at Five Colleges relies heavily on a strong,
ongoing communications network between the Five College staff and the
development officers at all five campuses, the deans of faculty, the chief financial officers, and the presidents. When the policy fails, it is usually due to a failure of communication somewhere within that network. The policy statement
to which we adhere is as follows:

> Five Colleges, Inc. observes a long-standing policy that all consortial approaches
> to foundations will be coordinated with the individual campuses. Any one cam-

pus reserves the right to request that the consortium not approach a foundation should that approach represent a conflict with that campus' own fundraising priorities or place the consortium in competition with the campus.

Coordinated approaches are planned through regular meetings of the campus and consortium foundation officers. Proposals to fund consortial programs are reviewed and approved by the appropriate Five College group—the deans of faculty for academic proposals and the principal business officers for administrative ones. In the case of large-scale proposals or approaches to major national foundations, the Five College board of directors (presidents, chancellor, and coordinator) are also consulted and their prior approval required. Often, when visiting foundations on behalf of their respective institutions, individual directors include approved Five College projects on their agenda for discussion with the foundation officer.

Five Colleges, Inc. raises funds only for shared or joint programs that are regarded as high priority by more than one campus and that no individual campus intends to develop on its own. Normally, any grant involving faculty members from three or more institutions is also submitted through Five Colleges. From time to time, at the request of the faculty involved or the granting agency, Five Colleges may serve as the institution of record for grants involving only two institutions. Consortial proposals are submitted over the signature of the coordinator as the responsible official and chief executive officer. If a grant is awarded, Five Colleges, Inc. becomes the agency of record and as such is responsible for the fiscal management and stewardship of the grant.

This procedure has developed gradually over the years, more through habit and experience than proclamation. Perhaps the most effective way to describe how the guidelines work is to cite examples in which the issues of competition, credibility, and stewardship were addressed.

Competition

Often our member institutions all receive the same RFP from a foundation. If each one responds independently, each is clearly in competition with the others, as well as with all other institutions invited into the competition. More often than not, our member institutions do respond individually to such invitations. Sometimes, however, and more frequently in recent years, the presidents or deans or development officers have suggested a consortial approach. At other times, the funding agency may have made that suggestion. In the last several years, our institutions have responded in a number of different ways, usually successfully, to the issue of competition.

Some years ago an RFP from a major private foundation was issued to liberal arts colleges throughout the country for improving undergraduate science education. Each of our four colleges (universities were not included) intended to respond individually. The foundation officers decided to meet prior to submission of the proposals in order to share their ideas and to ensure that the four proposals were distinctive and complementary. Each institution included a statement on how Five College cooperation would enrich the stipulated projects. All four grants were awarded.

A year and a half ago, we agreed on an entirely different approach to an RFP sent to presidents and chancellors of colleges and universities throughout the country. That RFP called for some kind of collaboration. Two of our chief executive officers sent the proposal to me with a note saying that Five Colleges should probably respond. After confirming with the funding agency that the consortium, rather than one of our institutions, could apply for the grant, we discussed with the deans of faculty what route they wished to follow. One institution, which was already well ahead in planning a project that would fit closely within the guidelines in the RFP, understood the advantages of a consortial approach. The deans, therefore, agreed that the proposal should come from Five Colleges but that one of the colleges should play a leading role in implementing the grant, if awarded. It was.

More recently, two of our institutions were discussing with the same foundation the need for increased training in and use of technology, and a third was about to submit a proposal for a similar project. The program officer at the foundation suggested that the projects should include institutional partners in order to increase the impact of the grant and suggested going home and talking to the other members of Five Colleges. The campus that was about to submit a proposal withdrew it and joined in a larger consortial proposal that incorporated all three projects in a more expanded, more inclusive program affecting all five campuses. Each of the three institutions involved in designing an initial project became the host campus for that portion of the grant.

We have learned that a strong and trusting communications network among the corporation and foundation officers can be highly successful in avoiding misunderstanding and tension due to competition for funds. A major misunderstanding did occur a number of years ago, prior to the articulation of our common policy. Five Colleges, Inc. had been awarded a challenge grant from the National Endowment for the Humanities (NEH) and needed to raise matching funds. One of our presidents was then in discussion with a foundation for a major grant to her institution. Assuming her role as a Five College director, she asked if the foundation would consider a grant to the consortium to help meet the NEH match. The foundation responded in the affirmative, a proposal was duly submitted by Five Colleges, and the grant was awarded. To the great dismay of all, the foundation had assumed that the Five College grant had priority over the institutional one and did not pursue further the grant to the institution.

This is not likely to happen again. We are careful to distinguish between a consortial approach and an institutional one, both among ourselves and with the funding agency. We often ask outright whether a Five College proposal would be in direct competition with an institutional proposal. Foundation officers respond honestly and then leave it up to the consortium and its member institutions to decide how to proceed.

Credibility

There are not many successful consortia with a long record of survival. Funding agencies are, therefore, understandably concerned about the longevity and viability of consortial arrangements, especially when they appear to be forged more by the expediency of an RFP than a commitment to cooperate. Questions program officers often ask are: Will the partnership outlive the grant? Are the institutions committed to the project? To what extent? Will they commit matching funds?

A number of years ago, the National Science Foundation was offering grants to cooperating institutions for equipment to enhance undergraduate facilities. Faculty members from our institutions came together to submit a joint Five College application. They each named the equipment they wanted at their respective institutions. The cooperative aspect of their proposal consisted primarily and solely of the fact that students at any one of the five colleges can take courses at any of the other institutions, that is, cross-registration meant sharing. We did not receive the grant, and the faculty members involved were rather chagrined. At a subsequent meeting, we discussed with the faculty how the proposal could be converted into a truly cooperative project rather than one in which each institution got its piece of equipment under the umbrella of a consortial proposal. The next proposal under the same guidelines was consortial; it included a new course to be developed jointly, with students moving from campus to campus using the equipment being requested in the grant. That proposal was funded and the course is still being offered.

Another concern that funding agencies have about consortia is the amount of institutional support available for a grant-funded project both during the grant period and after. Letters from presidents and deans help, but they must be individualized. Approximately the same letter from three or five or ten different people is not very convincing. Each letter of support from a president or dean should explain why the proposal is particularly relevant to his or her campus. Any mention of continued support for the project beyond the grant period is also a welcome addition. Even when matching funds are not required, it is helpful to demonstrate that the institution is willing to contribute time, space, or other resources. Some evidence of a long-term commitment from the consortium or any of its members to the project, the position, or the program is essential. If such a commitment is not forthcoming, the proposal should at least indicate what the long-term effects of the grant would be for the institutions and for the consortium. A newly shared position, for instance, can serve as a catalyst for innovation so that when the funding and the position end, the institutions will be further along in thinking and planning together for mutual advantage.

Stewardship

Five Colleges, Inc. is an independent, not-for-profit entity. We have our own business office and are responsible fiscally and administratively for the grants we receive; this means we also receive any overhead or administrative fees directly. The Five College business manager oversees grant budgets and provides our fiscal reports; the assistant Five College coordinator for program planning and development is responsible for stewardship and reporting on the implementation of grant-funded projects. She is often directly engaged with the project as it develops, serving both as a resource and communications link to the different campuses and parties. She also keeps informed about a grant-funded project after the funds have been expended and the grant period has expired, ensuring that promises made to the granting agency are kept and that the story of the grant's success is not lost.

Many consortia have very small staffs and do not have their own business offices, treasurers, or development officers. They are dependent on financial and development support from one of the member institutions, which means that grants to the consortium are being fiscally administered outside the consortial office. This can be problematic, especially when multiple grants are being administered by more than one business office. If possible, it would be beneficial to have one institution's office of grants and contracts take on the fiscal responsibility for all consortial grants. If this is too much of a burden for one institution, the home institution of the project director would be the best choice to provide accountability. Either way, it is wise for the consortium director or someone else on the staff to serve as liaison to the project directors and for the consortial office to have a full record of the grant history.

Even for consortia like ours that administer their own grants, there are sometimes troublesome complexities. It is essential to be scrupulous about record keeping and billing. If funds are being disbursed to more than one institution, stewardship can be a nightmare—lines of reporting must be clearly marked in advance and all expenditures verified by the appropriate person. Our recent grant for technology training has one person responsible for each of the different projects under the grant, and that person must sign off on all expenditures. It is much simpler, if not always possible, to have all grant bills come directly to one central fiscal office, whether at the consortium or one of the institutions. Billing several different offices and then transferring grant funds is simply too cumbersome and can lead to reporting problems when the time comes, especially when, as is usually the case, different accounting systems are in effect.

Every grant received and stewarded well is an investment in the future. Lingering doubts about the viability and dependability of a consortium can be reinforced by sloppy stewardship and reporting or erased with clear and prompt reporting. This is not an easy matter, however. Often, those responsible for implementing the project are on one of the campuses and do not report directly or even indirectly to the consortial staff. It is important from the beginning, therefore, to establish good and ongoing communication links with the faculty or staff in charge of the grant. It is too late to try to do so a week before the report is due.

Finally, success rests on good communication and trust—communication between the consortial staff and institutional staff and among the institutions. Frequent meetings, so people get to know each other, are critical. Electronic communication is a great boon, too; it allows the various offices to share information and serve as resources to each other. The Five College corporation and foundation directors meet almost monthly with the Five College development officer and are also in constant communication over e-mail. Their meetings have inspired the sponsored research officers (in some cases the same people) to meet as well and to put on joint workshops for faculty. Although Five Colleges, Inc. does not do individual donor fundraising, the major gifts officers sometimes meet together just to share their knowledge.

The investment in a development officer for the consortium has proven to be beneficial to the institutions and to the consortium. Without such a position, it is hard to imagine that we would be able to apply for or administer the number of grants we receive annually. Even without their own development officers, however, most consortia can pursue collaborative grants, relying instead on the help and collegiality of development officers on the campuses. There is no question that a cooperative approach to fundraising promises great advantages and attractions to the institutions and to their funders.

LORNA M. PETERSON is coordinator and chief executive officer of Five Colleges, Inc. in Amherst, Massachusetts.

One way colleges can approach cost control is by taking advantage of cooperative activities with other, similar institutions.

Cooperation for Cost-Effectiveness in Purchasing

Mitch Dorger

Each year my office receives calls or visits from college officials throughout the United States and from as far away as China who are seeking to learn about how a consortium of colleges is organized and operates. After a few introductory questions, the conversation inevitably turns to the bottom line. "Can any money be saved by operating within a consortium, and if so, how?"

This interest in saving money through cooperative operations is understandable. In recent years there has been a growing crescendo of voices across the nation calling for better cost controls in higher education. These are the voices of students' parents, of college and university trustees, and even of lawmakers. All are concerned that college tuition prices have grown at a rate well above that of inflation.

Top college administrators have clearly heard these voices and have tried to respond—but very real obstacles stand in the way of effective response. The cost of library materials, particularly journals—both paper and electronic—has been increasing at a rate three to four times inflation; furthermore, increasing governmental regulation and changing rules have increased the cost and complexity of doing business, and information technology has become a veritable "black hole" for funding in many institutions. Moreover, expectations are rising, both on the part of students and parents. They want more from the colleges and universities they select but do not want to pay more. Couple these trends with the need to provide facilities for growing enrollments and to provide competitive salaries for faculty and staff, and you have the makings of a financial Gordian knot. Increasingly, presidents and chief financial officers are looking to the administrative and support side of their institutions to find new ways of untangling the knot and meeting the cost-control challenge without adversely affecting educational quality.

In 1997, growing concern over the cost of higher education led Congress to charter a national commission to examine the escalating cost of a college education. The result of this congressional initiative was a report, released in January 1998 by the National Commission on the Cost of Higher Education, which not only examined the facts underlying college cost increases but also offered a number of suggestions for helping to control these increases in the future. Among the suggestions offered was that colleges and universities combine activities in order to reduce operating costs. In this chapter I take the commission's suggestion one step further by exploring some specific approaches to cooperative actions that colleges and universities might take. I also offer advice on how to avoid some of the obstacles and pitfalls inherent in initiating cooperative activities.

Before beginning this examination, however, a caveat is in order. Much of the information contained in this chapter is based on the experiences of well-established consortia of private colleges. Depending on the makeup of other existing or forming consortia around the country—public versus private or large versus small—it may be that not all of the options discussed here would be feasible for those consortia. Likewise, because the laws in each state are different, legislation or other regulations might be impediments to some of the alternatives discussed. These restrictions may not preclude implementation; but when such restrictions exist, implementation will require more effort and ingenuity than might be required in locations with less cumbersome restrictions.

Conceptual Approaches to Cooperation

The number and type of cooperative ventures that colleges and universities can undertake to increase their cost-effectiveness are limited only by the ingenuity of the managers involved. Space limitations preclude an examination of all, or even most, of these options. Instead, I introduce four conceptual approaches to cooperation, with examples of each. Readers can use these conceptual approaches and examples to stimulate thinking within their own organizations and consortia.

Share the Risk. The first of these conceptual approaches is what I call "share the risk," and if I were to recommend a first step toward reducing costs through cooperation, it would be in this area. Literally, tens, if not hundreds, of thousands of dollars can be saved almost immediately if ways can be found to share risk. Here are examples of areas that should be examined under this approach.

Property, Casualty, and Liability Insurance. Most insurance policies are non-linear with regard to the cost of insurance. Specifically, as the size of a policy increases, the cost of insurance decreases. For example, the cost per $1,000 of insurance is far more for the first $1 million of insurance than it is for the fifth.

This is partly because each policy has certain administrative costs built into the cost, in addition to the actuarial cost of the insurance. As the size of the policy increases, the administrative costs drop off. As a result, the cost per $1,000 of insurance for a $1-million policy will be markedly higher than the cost of a $20-million policy. The trick for groups of institutions wanting to reduce their risk management costs is to merge, with the participating institutions listed as individual insured parties, their smaller individual policies into a single large group policy to reduce the overall cost of insurance for all participants. This is possible if the parties are related in some fashion (for example, through a consortial agreement) and all agree to be covered by a common policy. One issue that needs to be addressed by the group is the deductible for each loss. Typically, even in the case of a cooperative policy, the deductible loss will not be shared. Rather, it will be the responsibility of the member institution experiencing the loss. Even so, there is still some shared risk with common policies. Specifically, if one member covered by a cooperative policy has a large loss, all the members will likely experience an increase in their insurance costs in the next policy renewal. This is an unavoidable risk but one that should still be well worthwhile, given the significant annual savings potential of a single large policy. As an aside: one way to reduce the risk to the group is to agree on common loss-prevention measures and perhaps even establish cooperative loss-prevention programs to ensure that the risk is more or less level among participating institutions.

Life and Health Insurance. Generally, the larger the covered population in a life or health insurance policy, the lower the rates charged for the coverage. Experience has shown that by pooling the employees (or students, as the case may be), a group of institutions can get a lower rate on life and health insurance than if the individual member colleges provide it on their own. Just as with the property and casualty insurance, however, there is some common risk. If one participating institution has a significantly different population (and hence a different risk profile) than the other members, it may affect the premium rates for the whole group. The caution, then, is that similar populations be insured under the common coverage.

Workers' Compensation and Disability Insurance. A number of consortia have saved a considerable amount of money by agreeing to purchase common policies for workers' compensation and long-term disability insurance. In some states such cooperative policies have been arranged on a statewide level. In California, for example, the Association of Independent California Colleges and Universities has arranged for cooperative workers' compensation and long-term disability policies that all member institutions can join (on a voluntary basis). In other cases, individual consortia have arranged such policies on their own. Some consortia have taken risk-management cooperation one step further by arranging both a shared safety program and a single administrative office to handle workers' compensation and disability matters. Experience has shown these groups that specialized management expertise in these areas can help keep policy costs down.

Share the Resource. The second conceptual approach to increasing cost-effectiveness through cooperation is to *share the resource*. Many parents teach their children that sharing is a good thing. Unfortunately, few institutions see the benefits of such a philosophy. Nevertheless, sharing resources can be a powerful way to stretch dollars. This sharing can take place in a number of different functional areas, and the resources involved can include equipment, services, and even people.

Equipment. One of the easiest ways to stretch procurement dollars is to avoid buying everything that is needed. In some cases, when cooperating institutions are relatively close together and have common requirements, it may be possible to share resources. This has been done effectively with high-cost but seldom-used machinery such as specialized equipment used in physical plant operations. This same concept can be extended to the stockpiling of high-cost items like electrical transformers. By agreeing to pool stockpiles, institutions can cut down on the need to stock all items individually.

Libraries. Another area for savings is in library resources. Most college and university libraries have reached the point that they can no longer buy all the journals, electronic databases, and other resources that their patrons desire. Some libraries are responding to this challenge by sharing resources, both physical and electronic, with other libraries. Through careful planning and cooperative acquisitions, coupled with appropriate sharing arrangements, libraries can stretch their resources and services to their patrons well beyond what their individual budgets would provide. Cooperative purchasing or licensing of electronic resources is particularly promising as an area for future cooperation.

Service Contracts. Many institutions outsource some of their services. These might range from physical plant services such as equipment maintenance, painting, tree trimming, pest control, or road paving to such areas as employee training, outplacement services, and so forth. Just as with the insurance policies mentioned earlier, it is easy to reduce the cost of service contracts such as for paving or painting by combining the requirements of more than one institution into a single contract. Combining contracts not only allows contractors to spread administrative costs, but also, because they are contracting for greater amounts of work, they can lower their profit margins somewhat. With regard to training, it is often possible to combine training for several institutions into a single session rather than conducting smaller, individual sessions at each institution. At a minimum, if outside trainers are being used it is usually possible to share (and thereby reduce) ancillary expenses, such as travel, by coordinating on-site training activities with other institutions.

People. Many institutions, particularly smaller institutions, cannot afford to hire staff to do everything that needs to be done. This often results in using outside specialists or consultants to handle the workload, which may not be the most cost-effective option. It might be far more cost-effective for a group of institutions to hire a single in-house resource and share that individual among institutions. Some examples of single positions that have been successfully shared by several colleges include risk management, recycling, safety, workers' compensation and administration, and real estate positions. The list is endless. The key is to find a common requirement among interested institutions that would not require a full-time staff member at each institution. By hiring one individual to serve the whole group, high fees to outside agents can be avoided. Consider, for example, an institution that takes in real estate as gifts. The cost of disposing of these properties through an outside real estate broker can be very significant, particularly for high-value properties. A shared internal broker could pay his or her salary through the proceeds of a single transaction.

Do unto—and for—Others. In any group of institutions, it is possible that one of the institutions will be in a position to provide a particular service to the others. This approach might be called a "lead college" model of cooperation, as opposed to the joint models outlined earlier. This is particularly true if one of the institutions is substantially larger than the others. For example, one eastern consortium includes among its members a large public university and several small, private institutions. In this example, the large public institution was able to provide central processing for a successful recycling program involving all the member institutions that saved the group thousands of dollars a year. Other examples of services that might be performed by one member for the others include printing, laundry, or travel management services. An important caution is that the Internal Revenue Service (IRS) has ruled that the provision of services by one institution to other, nonrelated institutions in exchange for cash payments constitutes unrelated business income, which is taxable. At least one consortium has avoided this problem by getting a private-letter ruling from the IRS stating that because they are formally related and cooperate in many areas, such cooperation does not generate unrelated business income. Clearly, because of the legal technicalities involved here, counsel should be consulted before implementing programs of this type.

Expand Your Bargaining Power. The final conceptual approach is the one that perhaps most people identify with when thinking about money-saving cooperative activities. Simply stated, buying in larger quantities can increase buying power and reduce costs for all concerned.

Utilities. One of the most productive areas for cooperative purchasing in recent years has been in the area of utilities. Two of the most lucrative areas for cooperative action have been natural gas purchasing and long-distance telephone service. In one instance, two large institutions located in the same city pooled the purchase of natural gas into a single contract and saved more than $1 million a year each, even though the gas was delivered to two different locations some twenty miles apart. In another instance, a group of colleges arranged the cooperative purchase of long-distance services at prices substantially below what any of the institutions could have purchased on their own. A major caveat in the area of utilities is that deregulation and increased competition in many utilities have made the future cost-saving picture somewhat murky. It may be that deregulation and increased competition will result in tremendous new opportunities for colleges and universities to form buying cooperatives. Or, conversely, it may be that competition will be so great that it will be unnecessary to form cooperatives in order to take advantage of the best rates available. Certainly, though, any list of potential areas of cooperation should include cooperative buying of utilities as a possible way to save resources, but careful analysis of current market conditions will be necessary before deciding whether or not cooperative action is prudent.

Bulk Buying of Supplies. It is still possible to achieve savings by buying in bulk, although this is becoming increasingly difficult. Computers, for example, can now be purchased directly from the factories at prices approaching wholesale, and large discount office supply companies and home improvement centers have made it difficult to save much money on other supply and commodity purchases. However, there are still opportunities, and this area should also be on the list of possibilities for any group of institutions seeking to improve cost-effectiveness. Creativity and an eye for "pop-up" opportunities are very important. For example, a bookstore purchased high-quality copy machine paper in railroad-car quantities and, in doing so, significantly undercut the price of even the discount giants. The key was having low-cost storage available to hold the material prior to sale. Two cautions in this area: first, be careful of quality. Some brokers purchase large quantities of discounted materials from manufacturers and then try to sell the material in quantity, promising large cost savings. Second, watch out for what I call the "requirements loop." Brokers trying to pull together cooperative purchasing arrangements frequently approach managers. The typical approach is to ask the institutions to specify what their requirements are so that the broker can then shop the order among competing manufacturers. The typical response from the institutions, when asked for requirements, is to say, "What is the price?" The broker then responds that the price depends on the size of the order, and this cannot be determined until the colleges come up with their requirements. This sort of tail-chasing loop not only can be frustrating, but can also result in a complete shutdown of the initiative.

One way to avoid some of the problems outlined here is to take advantage of existing buying consortia. Several states (or regions) already have an established buying consortium for colleges and universities (or other nonprofits). This sort of arrangement can offer the potential savings of bulk buying without the headaches of dealing with individual brokers. These larger buying consortia allow the purchase of things such as furniture, electronic equipment, and laboratory supplies at considerable savings. These arrangements are often funded through some sort of membership fee; therefore, interested institutions need to ensure that they will use the service in sufficient quantity to justify the up-front membership cost.

Services. It is possible to use the increased buying power of a consortium creatively. Even if common purchasing agreements are not used, the collective buying power of the group can be used to advantage. Four real-world examples come to mind. The first is for temporary services. Some established, temporary service agencies will agree to cut their margin somewhat in exchange for certain levels of business from a group or institution. For example, an agreement might be negotiated saying that, if a certain amount of business is achieved, the rate for all future business will be reduced. A second example is travel services. Although the travel business is becoming more competitive, some travel agencies are willing to negotiate rebates (or fee waivers) if certain levels of business are achieved. A third example would be moving and relocation companies, which will offer significantly reduced rates in exchange for group business agreements. Finally, a group of colleges used its buying power with an investment banking firm to reduce the fee charged by the firm in exchange for an agreement on the part of the institutions to use this firm when issuing tax-free bonds. Because all the institutions already used this firm, this was a noncontroversial way for the colleges to save 25 basis points (which is one quarter percent on the loan) on borrowing costs.

Software. Finally, it is sometimes possible to purchase software site licenses cooperatively that will reduce the costs to individual institutions. This software can range from small, specialized programs to large, sophisticated programs such as the entire student information system for a college. One consortium is currently examining the option of buying a common system for the group rather than having each member institution purchase its own student information software. This option could prove particularly important when there is heavy cross-registration of students between institutions, and it would be helpful if the cooperating institutions had common software or at least software that can communicate back and forth.

Pitfalls to Ensuring Success

If what I have described sounds obvious and easy, do not be deceived. The number of things that can get in the way of implementing what seems like the most obvious thing to do can be staggering. Here are just a few of the more common pitfalls of which institutions should be aware:

Organizational Inertia. Most organizations have built-in resistance to change, and colleges and universities can have more than most. This inertia, particularly at the implementing level, can often keep good ideas from getting off the ground.

Not-Invented-Here Syndrome. Another common pitfall is the not-invented-here syndrome. Some organizations oppose ideas that may be in their best interest simply because it was not their idea.

Differing Resource and Expectation Levels. A very real problem in getting a group of colleges to agree to cooperative service arrangements is that there are different levels of resources and expectation. One the one hand, colleges that are better off financially often have higher expectations than their counterpart institutions. Because they can afford better service, they are less willing to compromise down on service levels. On the other hand, institutions that are less well off financially are more interested in cost savings and are satisfied at a level of service below that of their richer counterparts. These differences can derail even an excellent initiative if not properly managed.

Another related problem is what the various institutions expect to achieve from the initiative; some will be satisfied with any tangible cost reductions, whereas others will only want to be bothered if there is going to be a large pay-off.

Favorite Sons or Daughters. Some relationships in colleges and universities are not about cost. They are about close relationships that have developed over time. These relationships might be with a very generous alumni donor or with a corporate sponsor that gives generously to the institution. One example involved a cooperative buying arrangement for computers. Although the group price was excellent, one member institution would never participate. It turned out that the nonparticipating college was buying its computers from an alumnus who was selling computers to them below his cost. In another instance, a group of colleges did not want to change their electrical service vendor because the current provider was a strong donor to the colleges.

Not My Ox. Cooperative endeavors sometimes mean that changes need to be made in either established external relationships or in the services provided to college employees. Cooperative projects can be shut down if one or more of the participating institutions see the arrangement as "goring their ox"—that is, they are the ones having to change, while another participating institution gets to remain with their original provider or service level.

Differing Organizational Cultures and Policies. This pitfall is closely related to the item about differing levels of resources and expectations. Some institutions simply have cultures, attitudes, or policies (or perhaps all of these) that are different from other members of their groups. One CFO remarked to me that his institution had never seen a low bid. They were much more interested in quality than in saving money. This comment stood in stark contrast to another institution in the same group that was struggling to make ends meet. Imagine the obstacles involved in getting two such institutions to agree on a single program or vendor. Another example might be if an institution has a policy of awarding contracts only to minority-owned businesses or to businesses within a certain geographical area. Again, such policies can derail cooperation. This can be a particular problem for consortia whose members include both public and private institutions, in that state rules and regulations may impede cooperative activities.

Ignoring the Human Element. If implementation plans do not recognize the impact of proposals on people, the proposals can quickly go astray. Two examples illustrate this point. First, if an office is already overloaded with work (as many are today), expecting that office to take on the additional responsibility for researching, coordinating, and implementing a new initiative almost guarantees that it will not happen. Likewise, the impact on other employees needs to be considered. A few years ago, there was a case in which it would have been cost-effective for a group of colleges to change their health insurance provider. However, to do so would have required many employees to change their primary physician because the physicians under the current provider were not members of the proposed plan. This resulted in widespread employee dissatisfaction, and the proposal was rejected, despite the fact that significant savings would have been achieved for all concerned—employees and institutions alike.

Trying to Cooperate in Competitive Areas. Each institution has areas it considers so close to its institutional essence that it will not cooperate in programs that appear to intrude into these areas. One possible example is fundraising; another might be admissions. Even though some cooperative activity might be cost-effective in these areas, proposals in them will be very difficult to get off the ground.

Successfully Introducing Cooperative Measures

No magic can be used to guarantee the successful implementation of cooperative programs. There are, however, some things that can and should be done when contemplating the sort of cooperative ventures that have been described in this chapter.

Start with Top-Level Buy-In. Presidential and CFO support of cooperative initiatives may not guarantee successful implementation for all the reasons outlined. However, not having this support right from the start almost guarantees an unsuccessful initiative. Top leadership must be fully supportive of exploring and implementing cooperative initiatives or the initiatives will stand very little chance of success. Innumerable obstacles can come up during the implementation of any cooperative project, and there needs to be enough "horsepower" supporting the effort to pull or push the initiative over these obstacles.

Be Incremental; Build Trust. Implementing cooperative programs is tough. As a result, there should not be a mad rush to implement too many things at one time. If there is, the effort almost certainly will become overwhelming and lead to failure. Management expert Peter Drucker once told a task force that if they wanted to do something important, they should only do one, or perhaps two, things at a time. That is good advice. A few years ago a major eastern consortium received a grant to explore cooperative activities. They examined a whole universe of potential options for administrative cooperation but finally settled on only four that would be examined in detail. This prudent course of action kept the workload for those involved manageable while permitting the group to gradually build trust. Trust is not something that comes naturally among institutions. It must be carefully developed and nurtured over time. This is particularly true if the cooperating institutions are just coming together and have not had the benefit of a long history of cooperation in other areas.

Be Patient But Persistent. Implementing cooperative activities takes time. There is inertia to be overcome, buy-in to be gained, and details to be planned. The programs that will be successful over time are those that are carefully and thoroughly analyzed and patiently implemented. At the same time, institutional leadership must be persistent in moving these initiatives forward. In many cases, those at the implementing level would prefer to see some of these things go away. Leadership needs to make sure this does not happen.

Do Not Try to Slay the Biggest Dragon First. In looking at the possible range of options, it might be tempting to tackle the toughest challenge first with the idea that, if we can do this, everything else will be easy. This is not the most prudent way to go. To the contrary, find some cooperative activity that looks relatively innocuous and start there. It is much easier to start small and learn the simpler lessons first, before moving on to the tougher challenges. This will help build a culture of cooperation among the participating institutions, as well as the sense of mutual trust that will be essential to "slaying the bigger dragons" down the road.

Avoid Competitive Areas. In any relationship between similar institutions, there will be both cooperation and competition. Agree up front on where cooperation simply is not going to take place, and do not waste time in those areas. However, try to be conservative in drawing up this list. There are a few areas that truly define an institutional essence, whereas others are not really central to defining the organization. Focus on the ones that deserve to be on the list, and watch for attempts to make the list too long as an excuse for avoiding cooperation.

Be Willing to Compromise. A willingness to compromise is essential to any cooperative venture. It is difficult to come up with a proposal for cooperation that will satisfy all the desires of all the participating institutions. Some compromise will be essential. This may involve the level of service provided, the cost of the service, or even the service provider. There must be a sincere commitment to the overall success of the group and a willingness to accept a less-than-optimal solution. This attitude must come all the way from the top levels of the participating institutions, or the effort could be in vain.

Do Not Get Hung Up on Unanimity. Do not be discouraged if every member institution does not want to be part of every initiative. There will not be unanimity on every issue. Accept it as a given. The basic rule ought to be that enough institutions should participate to make it useful for the group to act as a group. Some writers have tried to quantify this by recommending a rule of thumb of 70 percent of member institutions participating as a minimum level (Shafer and Reed, 1996, p. 51). That sort of precision may not be necessary. The key point is that good initiatives should not be postponed in an effort to get everyone involved.

Watch the Human Element. Ignoring the human element in implementing new initiatives is a good way to ensure that they fail. Be sensitive to those needing to implement new programs as well as those who will be affected by them. Whenever possible, search for incentives that make it apparent to all involved that the proposal is in their best interest. Recognize, however, that this will not always be possible. In fact, some people will lose responsibilities or individual office sizes might be reduced as activities become cooperative. In such cases, be as humane and compassionate as possible to those affected. This is especially important early in the process of implementing group cooperation. If people see other people being adversely affected by moves toward cooperation, future initiatives will be met with resistance.

Build a Cooperative Governance Mechanism. Cooperative activities do not run themselves. For every cooperative initiative, there needs to be a group of individuals responsible for ensuring that the program is running correctly and that all interested parties are being treated fairly. In the absence of collective oversight, suspicions can develop that some member institutions are being treated better through the cooperative effort than others. This will rapidly undermine even the fairest of cooperative undertakings. Having a cooperative governance mechanism in which all participants are involved in key decisions will help keep unwarranted suspicions to a minimum.

Share Costs Equitably. Included in every cooperative activity must be an equitable distribution of costs. All participants must believe they are being treated fairly. The trick, however, is determining what is fair. Equal shares of cost may appear to be the most appropriate way of sharing costs; however, this assumption needs to be evaluated carefully and discussed before implementation. Questions that should be examined include the following: What are the cost drivers in the activity? If one or two institutions drive the majority of the costs in the activity, there probably should not be an equal sharing of costs. Another question: Who benefits? If the benefit is uneven, costs should not be distributed equally. At the Claremont Colleges in California, some twenty different support services are provided centrally. Each of these services has its own formula for sharing costs. Some are based on student full-time equivalent (FTE), others on a combination of FTE and actual use; still others are shared on the basis of benefit. The important point is that cost sharing is nothing if not political. All participating institutions need to believe they are being treated fairly under the arrangement. If this sense of fairness is missing, the program, no matter how good it is, will eventually fail, as those who do feel they are being treated fairly will seek to go their own way.

Look Beyond Your Immediate Group. When looking to implement cooperative activities, it is natural to want to look to similar institutions. However, this shortsightedness can lead to lost opportunities. Consider city governments, school districts, or other nonprofit institutions in the areas as potential partners. Although this might lead to some increasing complications with regard to rules or regulations, it might also lead to exciting new opportunities. For example, I am aware of an arrangement in which a local school district obtains free access to college auditoriums for award ceremonies and activities. In return, the college acquires free storage space in the school district warehouse—a win-win situation for both. Likewise, it may be possible to make arrangements with an agency that looks totally different in order to achieve benefits. Power companies, for example, have occasionally recommended that colleges look to partner with something like a water district. The reason is that the electrical load distributions for these agencies are opposite. By combining loads, the partners might achieve the benefits of load aggregation without suffering the drawbacks of paying premium rates for increased demand during peak hours, which could be the case if two colleges tried to aggregate their loads.

Try Not to Reinvent the Wheel. Even though each set of institutions is unique, not every consortium needs to reinvent the wheel when it comes to examining cooperative activities. Some consortia have been cooperating for a long time, and others have gone through the start-up process recently. The Association for Consortium Leadership (ACL) offers an excellent resource through its many member consortia for any group of colleges and universities interested in exploring ways to improve the cost-effectiveness of their activities through cooperation. The ACL is a resource that should be consulted early and often by any group looking to move in the direction of increased cooperation.

Conclusion

Cooperation is a proven way to increase cost-effectiveness in institutional operations, and the suggestions offered in this chapter have proven themselves useful to others. I hope they will prove useful for others wishing to embark on this course.

References

National Commission on the Cost of Higher Education. "Straight Talk About College Costs and Prices." Report of the National Commission on the Cost of Higher Education, 1998.

Shafer, B. S., and Reed, W. S. "Consortia in Higher Education." *Business Officer,* July, 1996, 45–52.

MITCH DORGER *is executive vice president of Claremont University Center, the central coordinating agency for the Claremont Colleges in Claremont, California.*

A regional consortium in metropolitan Chicago provides an example of how sharing technological resources can advance state educational technology initiatives.

Statewide Consortia for the Use of Technology

Patricia Widmayer

How can a consortium of higher education institutions—two-year and four-year, public and private, major research institutions, comprehensive universities, and community colleges—successfully share advanced technology? Further, why would colleges and universities, with such diverse missions and only geography binding them, create a vision and strategy for working together? The experiences of the North Suburban (Chicago) Higher Education Consortium, one of ten consortia in Illinois drawn together by technology, provide some answers.

The Possibilities of Collaboration

The North Suburban Higher Education Consortium (NSHEC) began as a modest, voluntary collaboration in 1989 to pilot shared programs in Chicago's north and northwest suburbs.[1] The region extends from the city through the communities around O'Hare International Airport and along Lake Michigan to the Wisconsin border. Encouraged by the Illinois Board of Higher Education, which was exploring the potential of regional consortia, the six founding institutions (listed in the endnotes) organized to coordinate expansion in the growing suburbs.

A joint baccalaureate-degree-completion program on three community college campuses and a widely circulated directory of degrees offered in the region soon resulted. The executive committee's immediate objectives were to build relationships among institutional representatives, create a responsive organizational structure, and understand the cross-section of interests.

Several experiences led to the early and continuing success of the consortium. First, the partner institutions saw a common goal, prompted by the state, to create new programs to address the "unmet needs" for higher education in the region. They also were encouraged to try sharing resources to avoid unnecessary costs.

Second, the partner institutions agreed that each had identical status on the executive committee, sharing all decisions and dividing fiscal responsibility equally. When an institution could not or would not join a major initiative, the institution withdrew from the consortium. None were given differentiated status or responsibility.

Third, the institutions appointed executive committee representatives with sufficient standing in the college or university to carry out effective consortium initiatives and advance consortium policies. The executive committee was initially made up of vice presidents and is now a combination of vice presidents and directors. Each comes to the table with the support of the president.

Fourth, the partners immediately retained professional administrative support independent of any institution and funded the director's office through a combination of state grants and institutional contributions. Funding goes to one institution as fiscal agent under the day-by-day management of the consortium director. The consortium director reports to the executive committee through the chairperson.

Fifth, the structure is informal and organized around guidelines rather than bylaws. Committees and task forces are created, reorganized, and dissolved, except for the executive committee, as needed. The committee and task force chairpersons have continuing support as leader and spokesperson, customarily leaving their posts when no longer the representative of the home institution.

Finally, communications are constant among the consortium director, executive committee, subcommittees, special task forces, and others on the campuses. Before 1995, communication was by fax, express mail, and messenger. Today, e-mail is the mainstay of the communications network, supplemented by monthly agenda packets to the executive committee. A full description of the consortium organization and operations can be found at the web site [www.nshec.org].

The State's Commitment to Regional Consortia for Technology

For the first four years, while the consortium developed a strong, creative organization and promising programs, no major initiative emerged. Then the positive experience of NSHEC and two other regional consortia led the governor and the Illinois Board of Higher Education (IBHE) to a new strategy. The governor and the IBHE decided that the emerging regional consortia should carry forward the state's proposed telecommunications-based delivery system for higher education. The regional consortia immediately acquired a major purpose and a new level of significance. Few on the campuses knew about the fundamental technology, and even fewer were ready for distance learning. Still, the governor and the Board of Higher Education, seeing an opportunity, created the vision and the expectation for most institutions to participate.

The IBHE followed with guidance and administrative funding for the creation of seven additional regional consortia, bringing to ten the consortia covering the state. The state encouraged regions with community college districts as geographic boundaries. However, they set no structure. Rather, each organized around principles and partnerships suited to the needs and protocol of the region. A map of the regional consortia and a link to the website for each is at [www.ilednet.org].

An initial appropriation of $15 million funded equipment and installation of lines for a two-way interactive video network between the colleges and universities in each region. With three additional rounds of funding through 1999, the state appropriation ultimately totaled $60 million for a complex network of T1 (1.5 Mbps) lines connecting over three hundred interactive video rooms.

Courses, workshops, seminars, and meetings happen every day, extending higher education to underserved communities and using existing resources to support more students, faculty, and administration. The regional consortia interactive video network remains centered around higher education institutions, although some sites are at high schools, health care institutions, museums, and libraries.

Benefits, Problems, and Lessons

None of this happened without stresses, successes, major obstacles, strong sources of support, the withdrawal of some institutions, and the emergence of new players. The members of the executive committee dealt with the stresses and obstacles in the creation of a challenging initiative together. They "pushed the envelope" in many conversations, seeking to understand the technology. They worked through the organizational issues. Committees formed from their diverse campuses to think further about technical design, funding, programming, training, and campus support. Only then, after examining the many aspects, did they take plans and proposals to their skeptical campuses. Thus, they were fully prepared for the campus conversations and resistance that followed.

Working together, the leaders in NSHEC came to understand the problems and consider solutions. Faculty, administration, and technical committees spent hours and days designing, speculating, planning, questioning, and troubleshooting.

Further, the partners insisted on a collaborative infrastructure to support the initiative. They established a comprehensive "1-800 Help Desk," organized to handle daily problems with both equipment and personnel in a thirty-three-site network across eleven institutions. Training programs for faculty and technical staff address new needs and challenges in using the two-way interactive video network. A technology institute instructs faculty in the creation of Web-enhanced and Web-based courses to complement the interactive video instruction or stand alone. Seminars, workshops, collaborative research, and curriculum development are appearing on the network between the campuses.

Beyond NSHEC, some regional consortia have floundered. Some have been unable to create a dialogue or collaboration across sectors, viewing each other in a hierarchy rather than as responsive to different missions. Others have been late to hire an experienced administrator, thinking that the executive committee could sustain the initiative with clerical help and campus volunteers. Some have lacked the technical expertise to create or sustain a distance learning network to meet the goals of the initiative. Or they have received conflicting advice, making a streamlined network impossible.

What do the institutions receive from the collaboration? The principle benefits to the institutions are technology and applications that cannot be secured through independent resources. The principle disincentive is the "drag" of reluctant or turf-conscious institutions participating to obtain equipment for narrow campus purposes or to block the gains of others. The balance between the two depends on the consortium structure and the commitment of the partners.

Future Challenges and Opportunities

The technology collaboration between the institutions in Illinois is undergirded by a targeted goal, state funding, and the pressure of the state to participate. From this state's impetus and a strong consortium structure emerged an even more expansive technology initiative.

The next challenge for Illinois' regional consortia, beginning with NSHEC, is the creation of a shared high-speed backbone at speeds up to 155 Mbps and more. Such capacity is possible for most only through a collaborative effort. Carriers, equipment manufacturers, and integrators make far better offers—or even bids—with multiple institutions. Shared technical support and engineering expertise between the campuses add significantly to the project.

Conclusion

Faculty, students, and administration now look to the Internet and desktop videoconferencing for more extensive, flexible distance learning tools. Many see the potential of high-speed communications to support complex research and multi-institutional curriculum development. The state envisions university centers organized around technology to serve high-need areas across the state. And an Illinois Virtual Campus is on the drawing boards. The regional consortia are the pivotal vehicles for building affordable high-speed networks, acquiring advanced equipment, creating the needed technical support systems, offering training, and bringing people with ideas together.

Note

1. The six founding institutions for the North Suburban Higher Education Consortium (NSHEC) are DePaul University, Northeastern Illinois University, Roosevelt University, College of Lake County, William Rainey Harper College, and Oakton Community College. Barat College joined the consortium briefly, but withdrew with Roosevelt University when the state technology initiative began. National-Louis University and Northwestern University subsequently joined to bring the steering committee members to seven. Other partners in the technology initiative are the Chicago Historical Society, Maine Township High School, Elk Grove High School, and the Illinois Student Assistant Commission. The University of Chicago and the Museum of Sciences and Industry joined in 1999.

Reference

Horgan, B. "Cooperation and Competition: Case Studies of Academic Partnerships Using Information Technology." *Microsoft in Higher Education,* March, 1998.

PATRICIA WIDMAYER holds a dual appointment as director of the North Suburban Higher Education Consortium and manager of development and information technology at Northwestern University.

Educational consortia can benefit from becoming agile organizations (cooperative, flexible, and fast moving) and thus enjoy the benefits of sharing technological resources.

Technology, Consortia, and the Relationship Revolution in Education

Galen C. Godbey, Gerald J. Richter

This is the story of how a regional consortium of six private colleges and universities, in response to growing logistical obstacles to traditional forms of collaboration, initiated a process of experimentation with videoconferencing and on-line forms of technology-based collaboration. This effort has developed into one of the world's larger and more active distance learning and educational-resource-sharing networks. It is also the story of the growing realization that strategic relationships can strengthen educational programs and opportunities and that technology greatly expands the pool of potential partners by eliminating geography as a selection factor.

As with many instances of organizational change that yield new ways of organizing basic services, new capacities for production or new sources of morale, the emergence of the one-hundred-one–member Community of Agile Partners in Education (CAPE) out of the Lehigh Valley Association of Independent Colleges (LVAIC) includes elements of luck, false starts, entrepreneurial personalities, transformation, and continuity. From the point of view of the founding LVAIC consortium members, this process must not be seen as the repudiation or replacement of traditional forms of collaboration for which physical proximity is essential. Just as new technologies rarely supplant older technologies, the LVAIC consortium is as active as ever, supporting a wide range of academic and fiscally oriented services for its members. Even so, its members, individually and collectively, have permanently increased their actual and potential set of collaborators through CAPE.

As economic pressures increase, smaller institutions will learn to use technology to collaborate in an agile fashion, or they increasingly will feel pressure to retreat to "core competencies." Small departments with few offerings will be

New Directions for Higher Education, no. 106, Summer 1999 © Jossey-Bass Publishers

the logical targets of the pruning that springs from the analysis of these core competencies. The resulting narrower curricula would deprive students of both choice and intellectual excitement, and would erode further the competitive position of these fundamentally important but increasingly fragile institutions. Institutions must cooperate to compete and to share resources at unprecedented levels if they are to expand learning opportunities and customize learning environments for students.

Telecommunication and information technologies permit the sharing of intellectual resources at high levels of sociability and educational quality. Videoconferencing, for instance, closely replicates the classroom experience and is very congenial to the culture of smaller institutions, which equate small class size and close faculty-student contact with the overall quality of their educational offerings. However, distance learning technologies, including on-line virtual courses, satellite conferencing, and videoconferencing, have been used for the most part within higher education by large, multicampus universities or community colleges as extensions of the existing organizational model rather than as strategic tools for transforming the institution's approach to teaching and learning. For instance, although using technology to expand continuing education programs to off-campus sites, including corporate locations, is important, it is merely a geographic extrapolation of existing concepts and models or organizational structure and purpose. To date, these technologies have rarely been used to substantially reorganize the academic lives of the institution's traditional residential students, for example.

For these technologies to help liberal arts and other small and medium-sized institutions, they cannot be used as add-ons merely to extend the existing way of doing academic business, pedagogically and strategically. Rather, such technologies need to be incorporated into the life of the institution and made an integral part of a broader institutional strategy. We contend here— and it is the fundamental assumption of the CAPE consortium—that this strategy must be based on the rapidly emerging paradigm of organizational agility and virtual organizations.

The Agility Paradigm

American business and industry have responded to international competitive challenges by rethinking and discarding the mass-production paradigm in favor of the agile-virtual organizational paradigm. With its commitment to mass-customization strategies, agility is rapidly becoming the standard model for high-information-content manufacturing and other businesses that compete in international markets.

Agile organizations are cooperative, customizing, fast, and flexible. They understand the power of human capital and relationships. Products and services are means to ends, not ends in themselves; they are platforms on which enduring, strategically and economically important relationships can be built. In cultivating these relationships, agile service product providers think not only about customers and partners but also about customers' customers and partners' partners.

The virtual organization is the result of collaboration between two or more agile entities. A virtual organization combines the strengths of several separate, and sometimes competing, institutions to produce a quick and customized response to a rapidly changing environment. In the agile-virtual world, cooperation is a first choice, not a last-resort strategy. The agile-virtual organizational model has evolved rapidly in business and industry as a way for companies to survive in a radically changing environment that is no longer responsive to the structures and relationships of the mass-production organizational model, which assumes conditions of a large-scale demand for standardized, long-lived products and services.

To summarize, some of the key elements of the agility paradigm follow. In this modality, agile organizations strive to be

- Decentralized, concentrating on internal strengths complemented by the strengths of partner organizations
- Team-oriented, depending on educated employees who are flexible and innovative and empowered to take initiatives
- Organized for rapid movement from concept to cash
- Open and entrepreneurial, looking outward to partners
- Comfortable with simultaneous cooperation and competition
- Invested in relationships, seeking value-added solutions for customers and structured to provide customized response to diverse and changing educational needs
- Structured to provide customized response to diverse and changing customer needs

Agility and Education

The transition to agile-virtual strategies is as important for the educational sector as it is for business and industry. This is true not only in regard to an institution's continued economic and competitive viability but also in order to prepare its students for the twenty-first century. Students moving from mass-production-based schools to agile workplaces will suffer vocational culture shock. If we are to prepare students for the agile workplace and on-line democracy, schools and colleges must move toward at least a rough congruence with the agile-virtual organizational paradigm, seeking to add greater value to their services through the customization of learning experiences and environments and strengthening their own competitive position in the process.

Some specific implications of agility for education are

- Customized education
- Access to intellectual resources regardless of geography
- Elimination of institutional, sectoral, political, and geographical boundaries

- Cooperative enterprises and resource sharing with other schools, colleges, and universities as a *first choice strategy*
- An institutional culture that leverages the impact of people and information in the teaching, learning, and administrative processes through cross-functional teaming and decentralized decision making and accountability

CAPE's Emergence out of LVAIC and PETE Net

CAPE's organizational antecedents include the Lehigh Valley Association of Independent Colleges (LVAIC) and the Lehigh Valley Educational Cooperative (LVEC), a nonprofit organization founded in 1990 to bring together K–12 and postsecondary educators in the Lehigh Valley to develop professional and programmatic relationships.

In 1992, the funding with which the Lehigh Valley Educational Cooperative (LVEC) was started ended, and LVAIC essentially agreed to absorb LVEC's role of promoting cooperation and stronger professional relationships between K–12 schools and colleges in the Lehigh Valley. Further, LVAIC hired LVEC's executive director, who had substantial professional experience with cable television and videoconferencing technology, as a consultant to determine the potential of videoconferencing for supplementing LVAIC's well-established cross-registration and consortial professors' faculty exchange program. As road traffic in the Lehigh Valley became more congested in the early nineties, these hardy perennials of postsecondary consortial life were less and less convenient to participants. Of course, videoconferencing requires neither students nor faculty to move for purposes of course exchange.

These developments merged the long experience and steadily developing programs of a higher education consortium with the cross-sectoral mission of a collaboration between K–12 and higher education at a moment when telecommunications and informational technologies were being considered as an additional vehicle for joint action and sharing. The LVAIC board accepted the consultant's report on videoconferencing and charged its executive director and the former LVEC chief executive officer, now a member of the LVAIC staff, to raise the funds to install and experiment with this technology—a rare endeavor in collegiate education at that time.

It was decided that special-project funding from Washington was the most plausible route for so large a sum (videoconferencing classrooms at that time cost nearly three times their current price). However, six institutions from a congressional district with a brand new member of the House of Representatives were not likely to attract much support in a lobbying arena cluttered with petitioners. Consequently, following discussions at the 1993 Annual Meeting of the Commission for Independent Colleges and Universities (CICU) in Harrisburg, the LVAIC presidents invited approximately fourteen other presidents from independent four-year and public community colleges to join them and help finance the "fishing expedition for equipment money," as one president called it, in Washington. Ten of the fourteen invited presidents who attended the June 25, 1993 meeting at Kings College in Wilkes-Barre accepted the invitation to join the six LVAIC institutions in what would shortly become the Pennsylvania Educational Telecommunications Exchange Network (PETE Net).

The point not to be missed here is that PETE Net started as a grassroots effort that reflected the initiative of its members. It was self-generating. There was no state edict to pursue technologically mediated resource sharing, nor was state funding available when PETE Net was founded. Furthermore, the Kings College meeting could never have taken place were it not for the work of the LVAIC consortium—perhaps the only group of independent college presidents in Pennsylvania capable of relatively rapid, concerted action on a strategic matter—and CICU, whose regular meetings and role as a venue for policy discussions permitted the LVAIC group to expand its base.

PETE Net's job was to raise funds for equipment that would permit members to acquire videoconferencing technology and to use it to support institutional goals. However, while PETE Net (and subsequently CAPE) staff preached collaborative applications of videoconferencing and other technologies, institutions at first tended to operate out of the old zero-sum-game, stand-alone organizational model. A pattern developed. Control over the equipment was given to the dean of Continuing Studies to create niche markets previously beyond the reach of the institution in question. Throughout the remainder of 1993 and 1994, the staff worked with the presidents of the sixteen charter members on organizational issues such as adopting bylaws, forming the academic and operations committees, scheduling and conducting several technology demonstrations for faculty and administrative staff, and fundraising.

As time went on, schools, colleges, and universities that had acquired videoconferencing and on-line technology through their own devices sought access to the burgeoning PETE Net community and its resource pool. It was agreed that PETE Net should focus on fundraising for those institutions lacking infrastructure and that a new organization, separate from but allied to PETE Net, be established. CAPE was incorporated as a 501© (3), nonprofit corporation on December 23, 1994. The decision of the Council of Presidents of the State System of Higher Education to join CAPE in 1996 gave CAPE a tremendous boost by increasing its scale, pool of intellectual resources, cross-sectoral character, and geographical distribution.

CAPE is a support and consultative membership organization. It lacks—and does not seek—the authority to compel its members to collaborate with each other. Its job, in part, is to create an electronic neighborhood and to play host to help neighbors discover common interests and complimentary strengths. CAPE accomplishes these aims through its website, listserve discussions, faculty incentive grants, multipoint "get-togethers" for faculty and staff, training for on-line and videoconference technologies, free bridging for multipoints, "paradigm workshops," and other means.

Whereas most distance learning applications involving CAPE institutions are still unilateral—for example, an institution offering its degree program to a remote site—there is growing evidence that CAPE institutions are beginning to understand both the inevitability and desirability of collaborative uses of technology. As several institutions, acting unilaterally, attempt to compete for the same niche market via distance learning technologies, they come to see long-term advantages to both clients and themselves in pooling resources to share markets.

Important examples of technologically mediated interinstitutional collaboration among CAPE members include Duquesne University (private, urban) and Indiana University of Pennsylvania (public, rural) identifying complimentary strengths and needs in two fields of graduate study and then exchanging four graduate courses in each program via videoconference, with instruction going not only to each other's campuses but to off-campus corporate sites as well.

Marywood University and Seton Hill College (two small or medium-sized Catholic institutions) are collaborating with Indiana University of Pennsylvania on an undergraduate degree program in consumer science. It is likely that none of these institutions would offer this program alone. Through the use of technology, the public has access to three institutional locations distributed across the state, and students can choose among private or public, large, medium, or small institutions.

In March 1999, a team of eight faculty from six CAPE institutions, in partnership with a German governmental agency (which has developed a distance learning infrastructure in Eastern Europe) and Romanian and Bulgarian universities, began employing on-line technologies to teach global business practices to adult learners in Bucharest and Sophia. The CAPE faculty team members come from small or medium-sized institutions that, in the absence of CAPE's philosophy regarding collaborative applications of technology to build scale and expertise, might well have ruled themselves out of such globalizing activity.

These examples of cross-sectoral (public-private) collaboration are among many gleaned from CAPE's recent survey of its membership. This survey also found that a strong majority of faculty who use videoconferencing and other technologies for teaching believe that they are better and more creative instructional leaders as a result of their engagement with technology.

Conclusion

To close, we offer six propositions based on CAPE's five-year adventure with technology—our best effort to formulate a statement of consortial best practices relating to telecommunications and information technology for small and medium-sized institutions.

First, we need to stop talking about the technology revolution and start working on the *relationship revolution* inherent in these technologies. Technology must be approached as a tool or production environment for leveraging the impact of people and expertise within and across organizations.

Second, infrastructure without incentives and first-class training is guaranteed to fail. Training must address issues relating to both organizational paradigms and pedagogical environments. New technologies can renew and enhance teaching skills, and faculty learn best from each other.

Third, although the introduction of technologies is not sufficient to strengthen education, it is necessary. Technology cannot be viewed as an add-on to a fundamentally unchanging model of organizational life. It is transformative in its logic and must be integrated into every aspect of institutional life. As an organizing principle, it must be funded on a life-cycle basis.

Fourth, the agile and virtual use of technologies creates opportunities for small and medium-sized colleges and universities which were previously unavailable to them. Technology-based collaboration offers such institutions a historic opportunity to compete with larger or more affluent and prestigious institutions. Learning to use technology in agile-virtual ways, coming together rapidly to build scale and quality, will allow smaller institutions to compete with better-known institutions.

Fifth, the collaborative or consortial application of technology is inherently consistent with the cooperate-to-compete strategy driving the expansion of the global economy. Using technology to build collaborative programs and other learning experiences for students should be trumpeted as an asset for traditional undergraduate students because it predicts their future work environment; for adult learners, this approach increasingly reflects their current vocational reality.

Sixth, new institutional leadership is needed at small and medium-sized colleges and universities. Trustees must look for people with strong backgrounds in collaboration and technology. Drexel University's new Ph.D. program entitled "Educational Leadership Development and Learning Technologies" seems to have captured the heart of the new organizational dynamic and leadership imperative very effectively.

In short, best practices in technology, especially for small and medium-sized institutions, drive us toward new agility-based roles and strategies for teaching, learning, and organizational development. In this cooperate-to-compete environment, trust among partners will become the source of rapid and efficient exploitation of market opportunities, and consortia will help shift cooperation from the margins to the mainstream of institutional structures and functions.

GALEN C. GODBEY is executive director of the Center of Agile Partners in Education, Bethlehem, Pennsylvania.

GERALD J. RICHTER is chief operating officer of the Center of Agile Partners in Education, Bethlehem, Pennsylvania.

A Dallas–Fort Worth alliance is a prime example of how the consortium model can be used to achieve the required infrastructure for economic development initiatives.

Economic Development and Consortia

Allan Watson, Linda Jordan

With the almost seismic shift to an economy based on the rapid acquisition of knowledge and exchange of information, ongoing workforce education and training is critical to the success of American corporations in a global marketplace. Employees engaged in knowledge-based professions, especially those in the high-technology sector, must continually be engaged in the learning process. To attract, recruit, and retain these highly specialized, highly skilled employees, corporations must provide access to a vast array of education and training opportunities. An even more difficult task for these corporations is to support the workforce training initiatives with minimum expenditures dedicated to the internal administration of these initiatives. Increasingly, corporations are looking for a single-source solution to the myriad of education and training needs. Partnerships between business and higher education, orchestrated through consortia, provide a cost-effective solution while supporting economic development in a most significant way.

Workforce Training and Education: Fueling the Economic Engine

The impact of workforce training and education on economic development is often only thought of in terms of increased corporate productivity, profitability, and new-product development. These are tangible and powerful examples of positive training and education. Even more striking evidence of workplace training and education as a vehicle for economic development is Wall Street itself. New training companies and organizations are springing up to capture a growing market. Workplace training is itself now a product with a significant market.

Note the following: "Smith Barney advises its clients that a well-balanced portfolio should include investments in education and training providers. . . . Smith Barney bases its advice on these big drivers: the trend toward outsourcing; the evolution from a manufacturing-based to a knowledge-based economy; the ubiquitous nature of technology; changes in the workplace; advances in communications technology; the global economy" (Bassi, Cheney, and Van Buren, 1997, p. 46).

Whether delivered by for-profit corporations or not-for-profit consortia, workforce training and education has increasingly become the fuel of this nation's economic engine. Vehicles vary. From distance education to multi-institutional teaching centers, workforce training is an integral part of the economic development landscape.

Fueling Economic Development Through Distance Education

Pioneering new frontiers in distance education and collaborative endeavors for more than thirty years, the Alliance for Higher Education (a Dallas-based consortium of colleges, universities, corporations, hospitals, and other not-for-profit organizations) strategically links business and higher education through distance education initiatives. From its inception as one of the nation's first distance education networks, the Alliance has been and continues to be a major educational and economic resource.

Launched as the Association for Graduate Education and Research (TAGER) in 1965 by Texas Instruments cofounder, Cecil Green, to serve the ongoing education needs of his employees and other Dallas–Fort Worth companies, the Alliance embodies business–higher education collaboration to support economic development. Early on, Green and his Texas Instruments cofounders faced a dilemma if they were to make a success of their young company. They needed highly skilled and competent research scientists, engineers, and other professionals. In the early to mid-sixties, these professionals were not abundant in the Dallas–Fort Worth region, and to further exacerbate the problem, these types of employees were not being matriculated in sufficient numbers by area colleges and universities (Shrock, 1989).

As stated of the effort by one of his biographers, "An early question to be answered was how to bring students and teachers together. . . . At this juncture, one of Cecil's MIT fellow alumni, A. Earl Cullum, Jr., who was also a member of the TAGER organizing group, suggested that a closed-circuit TV could be used for intercommunication" (Shrock, 1989, p. 163). The TAGER Television Network, one of the nation's longest continually operating distance education networks, was thus born.

Understanding that a strong partnership between business and academia could assist Texas Instruments in recruiting and retaining high-caliber professionals, Green's vision expanded to serve many defense-related and high-technology companies throughout Dallas–Fort Worth. After more than thirty years TAGER, as a service of the Alliance for Higher Education, remains a strong tool for economic development, ensuring a well-trained and well-educated workforce for North Texas employers.

To date, TAGER has logged upwards of sixty-thousand registrations and has helped thousands of area engineers and other business professionals earn advanced degrees at the workplace by integrating the resources of area colleges and universities with technology. The Dallas–Fort Worth oil-and-cattle economy of thirty years ago has been supplanted by an information economy. Today, hundreds of high-technology companies call Dallas–Fort Worth home, and the need for ongoing education and training is increasing exponentially.

Access to convenient, good-quality higher education through the distance education efforts of the Alliance for Higher Education continues to fuel economic development throughout the region. Just as the Alliance explored the horizons of distance education with twentieth-century technology and cooperative partnerships with business, industry, and higher education, the Alliance now moves into the future with a new education and information network using twenty-first-century technologies: the Green Education and Information Network. Whereas TAGER offered one-way video and two-way audio connections, the new Green Network, with an official fall 1998 launch, offers one- and two-way video, two-way audio, and high-speed data transmissions capabilities.

With a fiber optic backbone linking Dallas and Fort Worth, a digitized broadcast signal, and the ability to connect with other Texas computer networks, the Green Network design will assist in cultivating the region's strongest resource—human potential—and ensure that Dallas–Fort Worth can continue to compete successfully in a global marketplace. Working closely with business and industry, the network programming mix of courses (degree, credit, and noncredit) is changing to meet the needs of the next millennium. In addition to more completely serving business and industry needs, the two-way video and data transmission capabilities also act to expand the resources of the more than thirty Alliance member colleges and universities by providing faculty resource-sharing opportunities.

The ripple effect of economic development is seen in the Green Network's ability to help Alliance member academic institutions recruit adult students who might otherwise be unable to pursue higher education because of time or distance constraints. Through distance education, Alliance member colleges and universities can serve more students without additional brick and mortar. Additionally, plans are under way to serve the larger community with literacy and job skills training at community centers and libraries. At the core of this future effort, historically underserved populations may access basic training and education, making them more attractive to area employers and adding them to the overall tax base of the community.

Higher Education Consultants and Workforce Development

By fostering business–higher education consulting opportunities, the Alliance for Higher Education opens yet another channel for the flow of information and knowledge to area industry. When an outside expert is critical to the success of a corporate project, product, or venture, the Alliance, through its Education and Consulting Institute, links business to the wealth of academic expertise of more than thirty accredited colleges and universities.

Through the Alliance Education and Consulting Institute, corporations find cost-effective consulting or specialized training and education solutions. Using a consortium such as the Alliance for Higher Education, which encompasses two-year, four-year, and research institutions, corporations save valuable time by contacting a single source. Experts in the fields of business, computer science, criminal justice, engineering, health care, hospitality, law, and virtually any other desired field can be located through one telephone call. The economic development factors of time and cost savings cannot be underestimated.

The ripple effect, again, flows back to higher education as well. Acting as consultants to industry, faculty experts can both increase their incomes and have a way to understand curricular needs directly from industry experience. This information can then be used by academic institutions to meet the education needs of business and industry more effectively. The beauty of this collaboration is that it comes full circle and provides economic development at the corporate, academic, and personal levels.

Building Education and Training Programs for the Future

Although meeting current corporate education and training needs is crucial, it is also shortsighted to simply meet today's workforce training needs. Although current needs must be met, it is equally important that future needs be anticipated in order to develop curricula in a timely fashion. If industry and higher education collaborations are to be successful, it is imperative that forums be created for productive interchange and planning.

To ensure that today's workforce training and education needs are adequately addressed through distance education and other delivery modes, the Alliance created the Metroplex Training Consortium (MTC). This group meets bimonthly to discuss the challenges facing today's training professional. Members share information and provide guidance regarding the education and training services needed by the corporate community. They also participate in special interest groups such as alternative training delivery systems, basic skills, bench marking, evaluation, and shared training. MTC members share common concerns, gather information, tour member company sites, and network to enhance training functions within their own companies. Through this forum, the Alliance for Higher Education stays keenly attuned to the education and training needs of Alliance member companies.

Meeting education and training needs of today while planning for tomorrow requires careful research, thoughtful planning, and the expertise of professionals in many and varied fields. The Alliance convenes these select individuals as "program selection committees" to provide guidance for new corporate education and training programs. This process ensures that marketplace and customer-specific demands are met with quality training and educational products that are relevant to today's business environment.

The Metroplex Alliance for Engineering Education (MAFEE), another Alliance advisory group, provides structure for colleges, universities, and corporations to work cooperatively to improve education related to the ever-increasing number of technology careers. Among its varied functions, MAFEE serves as another venue for assisting the Alliance for Higher Education in determining the most relevant technical education to be delivered to area corporations.

By convening engineering deans of Alliance academic members, interfacing with K–12 educators, and communicating with state agencies, the Metroplex Alliance for Engineering Education seeks to ensure that high-tech companies have access to a well-educated workforce both now and in the future. To prepare the future high-tech workforce, MAFEE also seeks to encourage K–12 students to pursue math, engineering, and computer science careers.

Adding Value to Workplace Training

Today, technical training that is developed in corporations is often at college-level standards. Corporations invest significant resources to develop and present information to their employees. Providing college credit recommendations for these courses is yet another way to affect the economics of workforce training and encourage employees to further their higher education careers.

In 1998, the Alliance for Higher Education partnered with the American Council on Education (ACE) to become the Texas affiliate for the ACE College Credit Recommendation Service (CCRS). Through this service, Texas companies can have their internal training evaluated for potential college credit. When the evaluation results in a recommendation for college credit through ACE, companies increase value to an already existing internal resource. Through the CCRS, the Alliance has not only increased its economic value to member corporations but it has again touched on economic development factors at the corporate, academic, and personal levels.

Multi-Institutional Teaching Facilities and Economic Development

Dallas, a shining example of corporate success and entrepreneurial thinking, has diligently undertaken downtown revitalization initiatives, but none may have been as daunting as creating a "living and working" environment in the center city. *The Dallas Morning News* in 1991 asked syndicated columnist Neal Pearce to study Dallas and offer his prognostication for its future. His study pointed to a glaring deficiency and an embarrassment for this proud city. It seems that Dallas was one of the few major cities in the nation without a four-year academic institution located within the boundaries of its central business district.

By combining the strengths of civic organizations, business groups, and academic consortia, this need was soon to be addressed with the state's first Multi-Institutional Teaching Facility in 1994. The economic development effects of this project have been broad and far-reaching; they have touched many sectors of the Dallas community.

Initially, civic and business organizations addressed the issue under the aegis of historic preservation and downtown revitalization. For city leaders, downtown revitalization was a focus. With the luster fading from downtown Dallas, they needed ways to attract new business to the central business district. With more than 117,000 (*Central Dallas Association,* 1994) employees located within the city core, the city also needed an incentive to keep current employees and employers located there. A downtown higher education center, as part of a multiuse redevelopment project to include retail and residential space, emerged as one viable solution.

For the city, the center addressed an important economic development issue. "The imminent opening of the downtown Education Center in the old Joske's store building . . . shows that downtown hasn't breathed its last breath and may yet find its second wind. In fact those who envisioned the center more than a year ago, as reported in the *Dallas Business Journal,* should be commended for proving that a new approach to downtown revitalization can work" ("Rethinking Downtown," p. 31).

Although city leaders took the lead on physical concerns—location, acquisition, renovation, and tax abatements—it became apparent that a unifying academic entity was needed to orchestrate the treacherous academic issues of "turf" and state higher education regulations. The Alliance for Higher Education was asked early on to manage this effort.

Through surveys and studies, the Alliance identified the student populations to be served. They included downtown employees, community college graduates (although no four-year institution was located in the center city, Dallas County Community College District's El Centro campus is located downtown), and minority populations residing in or near downtown for whom commuting to outlying suburbs for higher education opportunities was an impediment. Although pleased to support city economic and revitalization efforts, the five participating Alliance member schools were attracted by this cost-effective strategy for reaching underserved student populations.

By participating through a consortium affiliated with business and civic organizations, the academic institutions were able to expand their reach without building satellite campuses—a more expensive alternative than the soon-to-be Dallas Education Center. According to *The Dallas Morning News,* "Student access was the reason most university officials gave for their involvement in the education center project" (p. 30).

Although a small number of multi-institutional facilities were in existence around the country, there was no provision for this type of institution within the state of Texas. After much study and research, the Alliance coordinated the request for its five member institutions and presented it to the Texas Higher Education Coordinating Board for approval. This approval effected major changes to Coordinating Board regulations, which essentially eliminated "turf issue" impediments for future multi-institutional facilities in Texas.

The Dallas Education Center, recently renamed the Universities Center of Dallas, is in its fourth year of existence. It has often had difficulty coordinating varied interests and concerns; it had insufficient financial resources to market effectively at start-up. But now the center has more than one thousand registered students. It is a prime example of using the consortium model to achieve the required infrastructure for economic development initiatives.

Conclusion

Through workforce training and education programs, the Alliance for Higher Education continues to have both tangible and intangible effects on economic development. Through such projects, consortia can develop an image beyond that of doing "good works." It requires a businesslike approach and thinking outside the box. If they are to be successful, consortia-based economic development projects require much staff time and the ability to acquire the necessary financial resources. They also require that government and public relations efforts carry the messages to decision makers. A word of warning: consortia must count the cost of such projects in terms of their financial requirements and their public image and be prepared to position less-than-successful initiatives in ways that do not affect their credibility or bottom line.

References

Bassi, L., Cheney, S., and Van Buren, M. "Training Industry Trends 1997." *Training and Development,* 1997, *51* (11), 46.

Central Dallas Association, *1994 Annual Report.*

"Rethinking Downtown" (editorial). *Dallas Business Journal,* January 28, 1994, p. 31.

Shrock, R. R. *Cecil and Ida Green, Philanthropists Extraordinary.* Cambridge, Mass.: The MIT Press, 1989.

ALLAN WATSON *is president of the Alliance for Higher Education in Dallas.*

LINDA JORDAN *is director of marketing and public affairs for the Alliance for Higher Education in Dallas.*

Multi-institutional cooperation is now possible on an international scale; for collaborative international programs to be effective, they must have effective leadership, adequate resources, and sound partnerships.

Cooperating Internationally

Wayne Anderson

"The experience was transforming," one of the students reported after returning from an Associated Colleges of the South (ACS)/Rhodes College service learning program in Honduras. She talked about the profound impact of the experience on her life, on employment opportunities, and on her career plans. She now plans to look at international careers and perhaps those with a service organization of one kind or another. I also recall a student in our ACS program in Central Europe who indicated that his entire outlook on life and career had changed because of the international experience he was having. The intense experience overseas had enabled—perhaps compelled—him to look at himself, his capabilities, and his possibilities in new and important ways. I am sure the reader can recount stories of other students who have told of knowledge gained, networks established, and potential futures envisioned as a result of an extraordinary education experience overseas.

These examples and others reveal why the Associated Colleges of the South, like a number of other consortia, entered the international education arena. We wanted to open up challenging and rigorous international opportunities for students who were and are the central focus of our liberal arts colleges and universities. The international effort is aimed not only at offering new knowledge but at weaving together various strands of knowledge into broader, interdisciplinary contexts. The effort is about liberating students from narrowness of vision and intolerance of others and their views. The international thrust is aimed at providing liberal arts education as it ought to be, with classroom and out-of-classroom experiences that dovetail and reinforce one another, thereby enhancing the ability of students to prepare for an increasingly multifaceted and swiftly changing worldwide environment.

Like ACS, many groups offer international programs to provide valuable experiences and benefits for faculty, staff, alumni, and the community. They

NEW DIRECTIONS FOR HIGHER EDUCATION, no. 106, Summer 1999 © Jossey-Bass Publishers

exchange students, conduct joint research, sponsor conferences, and engage in service, among other activities. Whatever their composition, objectives, or location, they want to perform effectively. I hope that some of the lessons distilled from my experience and described in this chapter will be of assistance to them.

With the myriad of cooperative possibilities in mind, let us turn our attention to the matter of quality. How can we run such programs well? How can we make sure that our lofty ideals are not shattered by poorly executed operations? What are lessons to be heeded and pitfalls to be avoided in working together on international efforts? Some preliminary responses follow.

The Necessary Ingredients for International Cooperation

Among the necessary ingredients for a successful program, there must be support from the top—principally, institutional presidents and chief academic officers—and it needs to be very strong, clear, and unwavering. It helps enormously if those at the highest levels regularly send signals of support to their American and international partners, when possible inviting their international partners to visit campuses in the United States. All involved need to feel that the effort is an important one that justifies their time and energy.

The participating institutions need to feel that they have an equal opportunity to participate. They need to be among those making the key decisions concerning the program, evaluating various aspects of the effort, and deciding whether the program is to take new shape or be terminated. Perhaps not everyone will participate—after all, not every institution will supply a similar number of students on a study abroad or exchange program—but they need to feel they are kept fully apprised of activities, are able to register their views, and are taken seriously.

In the Associated Colleges of the South, we have found that not every consortium member wants to be involved in every program. Trying to cajole members into taking part in a project that is of limited interest to them makes considerably less sense than enlisting three-fourths of the membership, for example, who are excited about the endeavor and want to play an active role. The key point is to determine the critical mass—a number sufficient to supply the leadership and enrollment in a student-related program, for example—and then make an assiduous effort to achieve and maintain it.

Achieving extensive participation in a project rests on carrying out an effective marketing effort to participants, whoever they will be. And that means more than sending out attractive brochures and garnering a general nod of approval from study abroad directors or a scattering of faculty or students. After the group decides to proceed with an initiative, they must communicate extensively, using the full panoply of electronic and other communication vehicles. Drawing on the ACS experience, perhaps the best marketing occurs before the program is publicly announced, that is, as it emerges out of the planning process. Where programs have succeeded in our case, the individuals who created them have shared their interest and commitment with others on their campuses. They have become a powerful marketing force.

Among the best marketers of such programs, of course, are satisfied customers such as students who enroll in overseas efforts. Being able to demonstrate gains made and lessons learned is far more persuasive than making general pronouncements about the initiative. Students can play an especially effective role in attracting the interest of students on their own campuses and on other campuses as well.

A clearly delineated and understood decision-making process is also essential, from the outset of a program to its conclusion. This is particularly crucial in terms of relationships between United States representatives and their international partners. If the American contingent is expected to make decisions on certain kinds of matters, for example, this must be understood by the international partners, and vice versa. Many voices of experience suggest the value of clarifying the decision-making process and lines of authority ahead of time, that is, prior to an emergency in which there will be little time to consult or establish a decision-making mechanism.

Ultimately, programs must be of the highest quality, fulfilling the advertised objectives. This applies to any international program an institution initiates, whether it is a part of a consortium or not. No amount of transparent organization or sophisticated marketing can compensate for a program of poor quality. Moreover, one low-quality program can undermine the reputation of the overall organization, thereby affecting all its programs. If it means starting a year later and being more confident of the program, my experience suggests that it is worth the delay. It may be well worth waiting for effective leadership, adequate resources, and a solid partnership, among other necessary ingredients.

It is critical that sufficient funds be available, and these funds must cover an adequate time period to begin and test the project. Furthermore, it is wise to anticipate additional costs beyond those originally foreseen. I cannot recall a project in which unforeseen needs and requests have not emerged as the effort unfolds.

Where outside grants are involved, the participating institutions need to read all the fine print. Ideally, institutions should sign off on the grant and its various conditions, particularly if there are matching provisions. Sometimes it is difficult for a single institution to keep track of all these matters; the problem is compounded with numerous players.

If the project is a pay-as-you-go effort—perhaps a consortial summer program for students, for example—the terms of the arrangement need to be understood among all of the participating institutions ahead of time. For example, if a program requires a minimum of twelve students to pay the budgeted expenses, that number must be agreed upon by the sponsoring institutions. If there is a fallback position to a slightly smaller number, with expenses possibly paid from reserve funds, the institutions must agree ahead of time. Otherwise, there may be jockeying among the institutions to keep the program going for their own students—an unsettling and divisive experience.

Obviously, on some occasions a consortium may want to take a chance on a particularly enticing venture without being certain of the financial results. In such cases, it is important that the lead institutions and their counterparts understand ahead of time the worst-case implications. They need to ask: Are there sufficient reserve funds available? Are the institutions willing to provide a subvention to cover unanticipated costs? These questions remind one of the need to anticipate a wide variety of problems and issues that may emerge; laying out contingency plans that could be put into practice.

The discussion underscores the value of effective risk management. The risks identified should be those pertaining to the individual institutions and to the consortium as a whole. It does not serve the consortium well if member institutions protect themselves while neglecting the needs of the consortium at large.

Insurance should be available covering actions affecting the institutional representatives as well as any actions they may take. With individual or collaborative efforts, one would be hard-pressed to anticipate all of the unfortunate things that can happen, as our consortium's insurance representative recently informed us. Even those who work every day in the insurance field, she reported, are constantly surprised. Her remarks underscore the importance of taking the time and assembling the expertise to anticipate and manage the manifold risks associated with overseas collaboration.

Finally, I would like to urge institutions to come to grips with the need to terminate programs that are not working. Although taking such action is sometimes painful and can affect the reputation and prestige of the institutions attached to the program, such action needs to be anticipated and rehearsed. In my experience, it is easier to cancel a program if there are agreed-upon, measurable goals and objectives in place. Often, however, precise measurements are not available, in which case the potential for discord among partners can be very high. Consequently, the entire group must be fully engaged in identifying the goals of a specific initiative, reporting on its progress, and determining whether or not it should continue.

In noting the essential strengths or principles applied to multi-institutional collaboration, leadership is critical. On all sides—in the United States and abroad—partnerships need to search for leaders with international experience, expertise, perspective, knowledge of the specific country or countries involved, ability to deal with the groups involved, management talent, and basic competency in the use of technology, among other skills and talents. Fortunately, by mounting initiatives on a consortial basis, one increases the chance of finding individuals with such capabilities.

Pitfalls of International Cooperation

As there are elements essential to a successful program, there are also pitfalls to avoid in planning and conducting cooperative international initiatives. The first pitfalls are the opposite of the essential ingredients I have just mentioned. In other words, there may be debilitating problems if the leadership at the top is weak or mercurial, if the organization is unclear and decision making is not decisive, if there is unequal representation, and if planning is limited and uncreative. A mediocre program or one of lesser quality can spell disaster. Cooperating groups must avoid unanticipated and high risks of managing programs with insufficient funding. Further, if a group finds it difficult to terminate a weak program, problems are in store for the program involved and for the group as a whole.

Cooperating groups need to be wary of entering into programs for the wrong reasons, for example, because a specific opportunity happens to be there, or funding is readily available, or the opportunity may be a popular cause or fad at the time, or the project may look simple and easy to initiate.

Further, a group may seize an opportunity to provide a quick fix to a problem of one kind or another—an opportunity to solve an immediate problem or mend fences easily and swiftly. A consortium may assume that there is a ready market for whatever a proposed program involves or may find that there is an individual institution championing if not clamoring for the project. Perhaps nobody objects when a new idea is broached, suggesting that there may be no reason to hold back.

Another and often deadly rationale is that the costs to be incurred can easily be offset. Or the group may foresee budget relief produced by a project, lessening the pressure on institutional and consortial budgets. I would argue that these reasons for starting or continuing an international venture could produce deleterious effects for the participating institutions. None of the reasons substitutes for a methodical, deliberate, and comprehensive analysis.

Here is another caveat: avoid programs that are not congruent with the fundamental mission of either the participating individual institutions or the collaborative group as a whole. Not only can such ventures distract individuals in the group from their higher priorities but they can undermine the group's basic mission and greatly confuse its constituents. Also, the group could risk substantial funds, thereby jeopardizing its reputation and the reputation of its members.

Closely related to the last point is the need to avoid an intriguing opportunity—frequently a service program—that does not fit the organization at that particular time. However attractive and useful a program may appear, it might be ill-advised for the organization at a particular juncture, given its other competing and higher priorities. As difficult as it has been to restrain ourselves from pursuing certain cooperative projects of genuine importance and promise, my colleagues and I have done so because the staff would have been spread too thinly and other initiatives would have been given short shrift.

Another pitfall is a limited market for the contemplated project. A study abroad project may not have a sufficient market to justify the critical planning, advertising, and implementing of the program. An exchange program may be unlikely to draw students from one partner or another. A development project may have some appeal and might be eminently feasible, but it may have little impact in terms of the broader clientele or market. It may offer limited promise as a model for the broader society.

The Associated Colleges of the South tries to avoid programs that are limited to a short-term impact. In our case, we strive to forge the connections and networks that can generate long-term benefits. We entered into exchanges in Central Europe, for example, looking ahead to the possibility that exchanges of faculty and students, collaborative library projects, exchanges of administrative expertise, and other cooperation might develop. Although I am not denying the value of test cases or experiments, I am suggesting that focusing only on short-term opportunities may limit one's horizons and possibilities.

Another land mine is a sense of rising expectations—the case of a cooperative program generating expectations that are unlikely to be fulfilled. Although this tendency may be difficult to contain, and no wants to discourage the creative juices from flowing, it helps to be alert to such a possibility. Otherwise, the result can be widespread disappointment and dismay. The groups need to pinpoint and agree on the expectations early in the program and beware of letting them get out of hand as the effort unfolds.

Also to be avoided are partners that do not suit or complement one another. They may see the project through different lenses; they may communicate in vastly different ways; there may be implicit and explicit goals that clash; the talents may not dovetail in ways that strengthen the overall collaborative pattern; there may not be the same resolve to overcome cultural and other differences—and these differences may be too vast to overcome for the project at hand. Groups need to analyze each other very thoroughly.

Conclusion

Richard M. Krasno, former president of the Institute of International Education, has made some important observations about educational exchanges that could apply to other partnerships as well (Krasno, 1994, pp. 35–36). He observed that educational exchanges build the human capital needed to combat poverty and manage the complex problem of modernization, "foster informed international dialogue and greater mutual understanding," and create "enduring links among individuals and institutions." He wrote about investing in people in a way that "encourages the forging of creative, multilateral partnerships and takes advantage of the full range of intellectual and scientific talents worldwide. Educational exchange, by its very nature, is a premier means for accomplishing these goals." Krasno observed that, "the challenges loom large, but present an unprecedented opportunity for international education to help build a more peaceful, prosperous, and secure world." Let us hope that partnerships, small and vast, can produce such extra-ordinary results.

Reference

Krasno, R. M. "International Education: Challenges for the 21st Century." In *The Power of Education Exchange*. New York: Council on International Education Exchange, 1994, 35–36.

WAYNE ANDERSON *is president of the Associated Colleges of the South, Decatur, Georgia.*

Small colleges can be effective in consortial arrangements because they are, of necessity, more interdependent and are often less fiercely competitive than larger institutions, thus making better personal relationships possible.

What Small Colleges Can Do Together

Anneke J. Larrance

Others have written about collaborative activities that are suitable for large educational consortia (see Blumenstyk, 1990; Fehnel, 1982; Martin, 1981; Neal, 1984; Neal, 1985; Stanley, 1993; Watkins, 1991; Wilson, 1992), but little has been written about the niche occupied by small colleges that join together to form small consortia. It is useful for three to five small colleges to come together in a consortial arrangement; important and valuable programs and collaborations can result. Even though they are small in numbers and budget, such consortia strongly affect local higher education.

In fact, some collaborative efforts are suited for small consortia precisely because of the size of the consortium. These positive experiences provide the framework for this discussion of the accomplishments of one such small college consortium—Associated Colleges of the St. Lawrence Valley, in northern New York.

Different Kinds of Consortia

From the beginnings in 1925 of the Claremont Colleges in California, various kinds of consortial agreements have emerged and prospered. Consortia of different sizes, with different reasons for collaborating, with homogeneous or heterogeneous populations, and with varying sizes of operating budgets are all valuable for different organizational purposes in higher education.

As an example of a large consortium with a heterogeneous population and large operating budget, the Alliance for Higher Education has twenty-seven principal participants (all colleges and universities in Texas) and twenty-three associated participants (corporations, public libraries, a medical center, and industry), with an operating budget of $2.5 million.

The Coalition of Christian Colleges and Universities—a specific-mission consortium with eighty-nine members—focuses "on helping Christian colleges and universities better fulfill their mission to effectively integrate biblical faith, scholarship and service" (*Consortium Directory,* 1997 p. 25).

In contrast, the Associated Colleges of the St. Lawrence Valley (ACSLV) has four college and university members and an operating budget of less than $65,000. The consortium's purposes are to expand educational opportunities to students, to share resources, to avoid unnecessary duplication, to make full use of faculty talents, and to provide solutions and innovative programs.

Small consortia like ACSLV are much different from the Alliance for Higher Education. Yet the accomplishments of small consortia are rarely highlighted in print or the media, and we do not stop to notice their importance. Small colleges in consortia are an overlooked success story.

Background of One Small Consortium

The Associated Colleges of the St. Lawrence Valley was granted a provisional charter in 1970 and incorporated in 1974. The consortium includes four small college and university members: Clarkson University, St. Lawrence University, State University of New York at Potsdam, and State University of New York College of Technology at Canton. These four campuses are located within twelve miles of each other in two villages in northern New York near the Canadian border, and their combined undergraduate and graduate student enrollment is under ten thousand.

Consortia enjoyed a growth surge in the late sixties and early seventies (Patterson, 1974), predicated on the hope and belief that organizations like these would help solve some resource problems and increase the viability of colleges and universities. The early ACSLV consortium flourished; its staff, with enthusiastic support from the member college presidents and grant money, coordinated numerous programs and opportunities for collaboration.

However, in 1992 Associated Colleges of the St. Lawrence Valley became a smaller consortium. Today it has the same four educational institutional members, but the consortium has a part-time staff and a modest budget generated by member dues and the indirect costs from a long-standing grant.

Factors that Create Successful Consortial Cooperation

Large grants, shared technical infrastructure, and bulk buying do not measure success at ACSLV. Success is measured by the impact of the faculty development conferences held each year, by the working cooperation within the four instructional technology divisions, by the community and campus involvement with the performances and residency activities of our Performing Arts Series, by the collegiality and collaboration of the members of the Multicultural Alliance of Northern New York (MANNY), and by the cooperation that is evident among the registrars and librarians. Success may also eventually be measured in terms of savings, as a new initiative involving a coordinated effort with mail and duplicating services is being investigated.

No matter how success is measured, small consortia are vital. Both large and small consortia experience similar needs for success (goals and vision, for example, are important in all consortia), but in the following sections are requirements for success that apply particularly to small consortia.

The Need for Interdependence

Johnson (1988) asserts that "one of the challenges for the consortium leader is to develop an entrepreneurial and innovative spirit that will thrive in such [a competitive] environment" (p. 194). But how can institutions be interdependent when competition exists?

Kim Strosnider (1998) reminds us that today's focus in higher education is to cut costs through cooperative efforts in order to save money and ultimately reduce tuition. This demand to cut costs creates an absolute need for small consortia to support each another. Therefore, if competition is evident in small colleges in consortia (and it is), that competition is less fierce because of the greater need for interdependence that is fostered by today's educational needs.

Perhaps because the need for interdependence (and survival in today's educational milieu) is better articulated at small institutions, it precludes the competitive drive. The small schools at ACSLV (two public and two private) do not compete for the same students. Their need for interdependence is greater because of the "outside" competitive climate in the higher education community. The lack of fierce competition and a heightened sense of interdependence among the small college members may also be the product of a consortium director's skills. Given the demands placed on the resources of a small consortium, it is a blessing that direct competition is less intense and interdependence can be nourished.

For example, this need for greater interdependence has led Associated Colleges of the St. Lawrence Valley to hire a consultant to look at the mail and print operations at the four colleges. Can combining the four separate operations save money? What will happen to customer service? Do the peak needs for printing and mailing (for example, admission pieces) all fall at the same time of year? Would this collaboration, if it takes place, affect the two local post offices? These are questions that need to be answered, but without a consortial effort and an articulated interdependence the exploration would never happen.

Interpersonal Relationships

A second reason for the success of small consortial colleges is that committee and task force participants who live and work in the same community often know one another outside the consortium. Good working relationships and collaborations are more easily formed because of these interpersonal relationships.

Interpersonal relationships add to the vitality of the international student orientation and leadership committee of the Associated Colleges of the St. Lawrence Valley—a group that accomplishes an enormous amount of significant work. This committee of four plans and organizes an annual orientation for seventy-five new international students every year. In the past, they planned and executed a leadership education retreat and yearlong series of seminars for international students. Presently, they are engaged in a collaboration that will encourage coordination of multicultural programming on the four campuses. The members know and interact with each other outside their consortium responsibilities; consequently this committee manifests an extra willingness to share ideas, concepts, successes, failures, and future opportunities. I am convinced that the work of this consortial group has been extended, expanded, and strengthened because of personal connections outside the work arena.

Involvement of College Presidents

Patterson (1974) reports: "In the smaller consortium the importance of presidential commitment is proportionally large, and most cannot survive a negative shift by any member institution" (p. 13). At the Associated Colleges of the St. Lawrence Valley, there is involvement in the consortium from the top down. The college presidents are the board members, and their interest and demonstrated support encourage faculty and staff to become involved in collaborative efforts.

Any new program or cooperative effort is more easily pursued at the small rather than the large consortial level because it can be quickly organized from the top down without the mediation and paybacks that may be involved in large board politics. As Patterson (1974) points out, large governing bodies have difficulties reaching consensus. Smallness generally precludes multilayered bureaucracy, thus making it easier for the executive director to lead.

The Performing Arts Series (PAS) of the ACSLV is a good example of success resulting from presidential involvement. Member presidents recognized that what is good and profitable for the individual institutions and consortium would also be profitable and good for the local community. Our PAS was thus designed to serve the community as well as the students and staff.

Specifically arranged to bring "culture" to rural, isolated northern New York, the series was originally well supported by grant money and drew big-name entertainers to the four campuses. The grant money ensured that the ticket prices were kept low while the quality and appeal of the entertainers remained high. Many community members attended these performances along with students, faculty, and staff. Participation at all levels was increased because access to events was inexpensive.

In 1995–96, the Performing Arts Series became devoted to multiculturalism and now celebrates diversity through the arts. Residency activities are a large part of the series, and the community as well as those who are institutionally affiliated can see and interact with performers on an informal basis. In this case, presidential involvement led to a campus and community opportunity that has strengthened community ties and increased visibility.

Critical Mass for Change

It is difficult for two or three staff or faculty members to elicit lasting changes or cooperation on individual campuses, but on small campuses this may be all that are interested in a particular concept or plan. Even if the idea and resulting plan are brilliant, lack of local resources and energy may spell the failure of a well-conceived idea.

Consortial work is important in small consortia because small colleges alone simply do not have the human critical mass to effect change; they must create a critical mass by joining together. Baus (1988) notes that "Cooperation must be developed out of a sense of strength and gain on the part of collaborating institutions" (p. 26). By combining resources from four campuses, we have formed a critical mass of opinions and people who can make a difference.

For example, on their own, the multicultural professionals and those who work with internationals and students of color do not have enough mass on any one of our campuses in rural New York to effect change. However, by joining together at the consortial level, they can network and provide greater opportunities for themselves and the students they represent.

MANNY was organized in 1993. MANNY now has fifty-five members who meet four times each academic year. The focus is on the professionals and the students they represent, so the directors of multiculturalism, Collegiate Science and Technology Educational Program directors, Higher Education Opportunity Program coordinators, and directors of Native American organizations are among the members.

The goals of MANNY are to provide opportunities for support and networking among professionals committed to multicultural development, to share information, and to coordinate multicultural events within our consortium. MANNY members are interested in efforts to retain staff of color in this rural location and have coordinated efforts to attract and keep newly hired minority faculty and staff.

Related to this development, the Associated Colleges of the St. Lawrence Valley received a small grant to facilitate organization among consortial student groups for coordinating multicultural programming on the four campuses. Campus presidents designated discretionary funds so the organization could organize and schedule transportation to multicultural events on the four campuses. What an accomplishment for a group of like-minded people who did not have the critical mass on any one campus to make an appreciable difference!

Low Cost

Coordination at the small consortial level is inexpensive. Dues are kept to a minimum (under $10,000 at Associated Colleges of the St. Lawrence Valley) because we do not have a large staff or expensive and cumbersome programs to support.

Low-cost programs with high impact are important for small consortia, and cross-registration is an excellent example. ACSLV has a strong cooperative course exchange, and minimal expense is expended to coordinate this program. Our cross-registration allows full-time degree-seeking undergraduates and staff to take two courses per academic year at another institution on a space-available basis. Fees are not charged and the paperwork involved is simple.

Courses regularly drawing students from member campuses include fine arts, elementary education, Reserve Officer Training Corps (ROTC), economics, and marketing. This course exchange is an inexpensive way for these four small colleges and universities to serve their students in ways that would not otherwise be economically feasible.

Caveats

Small consortia suffer from the same concerns that plague large consortia. Committee members who are unwilling or unable to collaborate, an annual budget that must be balanced, deadlines to be met, existing programs to maintain, and new ideas to inaugurate affect the work of small consortia too.

Although there are advantages for small institutions in consortial agreements, limited staff resources and budgetary constraints mean that mistakes at small consortia are costly and deadly. In fact, there appears to be an added incentive to be highly selective in the areas of pursued cooperation and an increased determination that the selected areas of cooperation be successful.

The directors of small consortia must be carefully chosen. As with any consortium director, the demands of the job are high, but the director of a small consortium faces special concerns. Conversations, regular contact, and exchanges of ideas with peers are opportunities that directors of smaller consortia frequently lack. If peer contact is not readily available, then directors of small consortia must seek these opportunities outside the organization in order to grow professionally and to maintain their enthusiasm, focus, and vision.

The director of a small consortium must be a master of collaboration. The director usually convenes the task forces and committees. He or she must be willing to lay the groundwork for collaboration—modeling the cooperative spirit necessary to achieve success and directing the early conversations so that they remain focused and free of turf considerations. The director sustains the relationships and provides continuity.

Small consortia probably should not attempt some of the ventures that large institutions and associate members from the public sector do. Examples are purchasing joint health insurance or worker's compensation, pursuing large grants, sponsoring multiple-day conferences, or coordinating a joint academic department. Lobbying state and local governmental bodies is usually beyond the resources of small consortia as well. Some ideas are not feasible because the savings are not worth the cost of coordination; others are not because of staff and resource constraints.

Unless small consortia are striving to become big consortia, they should not stretch resources by attempting too much. Overextension of resources leads to fragmentation, unfinished or ill-conceived programs, and director turnover.

Conclusion

Important opportunities exist for colleges in a small consortial arrangement. Small college consortia cannot accomplish all the things that make large consortia successful, but considerable effective and important collaboration can be realized.

References

Baus, F. "The Third-Party Role." In D. Neal (ed.), *Consortia and Interinstitutional Coopera-tion.* Riverside, N.J.: Macmillan, 1988.

Blumenstyk, G. "Public-Private Group Sought in Portland to Help Colleges Meet Demands Through Coordination Instead of Expansion." *Chronicle of Higher Education,* Sept. 12, 1990, A23–24.

Consortium Directory. Norfolk, Va.: Association for Consortium Leadership, 1997.

Fehnel, R. "The National University Consortium." *Continuing Higher Education,* Fall 1982, *30* (4), 21–23.

Johnson, D. A. "The Limits of Cooperation." In D. Neal (ed.), *Consortia and Interinstitutional Cooperation.* Riverside, N.J.: Macmillan, 1988.

Martin, D. "The Academic Consortium: Limitations and Possibilities." *Educational Record,* Winter, 1981, 36–39.

Neal, D. "New Roles for Consortia." *Planning for Higher Education.* Winter, 1984, *12* (2), 23–31.

Neal, D. "Interinstitutional Cooperation in Continuing Education." *Continuing Higher Education,* Spring 1985, *33* (2), 11–14.

Patterson, F. *Colleges in Consort: Institutional Cooperation Through Consortia.* San Francisco: Jossey-Bass, 1974.

Stanley, R. "Retirement and Health Insurance." *Community College Journal,* Feb./Mar. 1993, *63* (4), 36–39.

Strosnider, K. "Collaborating to Cut Costs." *Chronicle of Higher Education,* May 29, 1998, A41–42.

Watkins, B. "18 Universities Join Effort to Offer Bachelor's Degrees in Management, Entirely Through Cable Television." *Chronicle of Higher Education,* Sept. 25, 1991, A18.

Wilson, D. "Research Libraries Group Seeks New Focus and New Members." *Chronicle of Higher Education,* Jan. 22, 1992, A21–22.

ANNEKE J. LARRANCE is executive director of Associated Colleges of the St. Lawrence Valley, Potsdam, New York.

ANNOTATED BIBLIOGRAPHY

The works in this bibliography represent the major historical and contemporary issues and themes pertinent to interinstitutional collaboration and consortia.

Grupe, F. *Interinstitutional Cooperation, Consortia, and Regionalism: Comprehensive Bibliography,* No. 3 (with citations to 1983). Kansas City: Council for Interinstitutional Leadership, 1984.
    A scholar, leader, and prolific author on interinstitutional cooperation and consortia, Grupe has cited hundreds of books, articles, and research papers.

Keim, M. B. *Interinstitutional Cooperation and Consortia: Bibliography Update* (with citations to 1996). Norfolk, Va.: Association for Consortium Leadership, 1996.
    This bibliography contains books, book chapters, journal articles, dissertations, reports, conference presentations, and articles in *The Chronicle of Higher Education* from 1983 to 1996. A compliment to Grupe's biography, Keim also includes citations that were published before 1984 and not found in his earlier work.

Poland, M. W. "Bibliography." In D. Neal (ed.), *Consortia and Interinstitutional Cooperation.* New York: The American Council on Education/Macmillan, 1988.

Books

Bridges, D. (ed.). *Consorting and Collaborating in the Education Marketplace.* Bristol, Pa.: Falmer Press, 1996. (ED 394 174)
    The book was written in Great Britain; the authors discuss their participation in collaborative arrangements, including consortia, which emerged following the development of the education marketplace. The book's fourteen chapters follow two themes, eight of which deal with the different types of collaborative arrangements, and six address conditions within which successful consortia operate.

Donovan, G. F. (ed.). *College and University Interinstitutional Cooperation.* Washington, D.C.: The Catholic University of America Press, 1964.
    This book represents one of the earliest collections of discussions on the potential within and barriers to interinstitutional collaboration. Although dated, the issues remain contemporary.

Neal, D. C. (ed.). *Consortia and Interinstitutional Cooperation.* New York: The American Council on Education/Macmillan, 1988.

Neal and the fourteen collaborating authors provide evidence of how interinstitutional cooperation through a consortium can lead to better-managed and more successful institutions. The authors (mostly executive directors of consortia) share their views on consortial activities ranging from joint academic programs to partnerships with the business community. The volume also includes a bibliography, many entries of which contain brief annotations.

Patterson, F. *Colleges in Consort*. San Francisco: Jossey-Bass, 1974.

Regarded by many as required reading for anyone involved in a consortium, this book presents a carefully constructed, sometimes critical and yet realistic picture of consortia in higher education. The year-long study involved on-site visits of twenty-six of the sixty-five consortia in the country, extensive archival analyses, and interviews with those involved with the consortia phenomena during the late 1960s to early 1970s.

Directory

Dotolo, L. G., and Beltz, N. V. *Association for Consortium Leadership Directory, 30th Anniversary Edition*. Norfolk, Va.: Association for Consortium Leadership, 1997.

This directory, which may be used as a reference tool for those interested in collegiate cooperation and the academic consortial movement, underscores the importance and magnitude of the cooperation that currently exists in higher education. This works contains all pertinent information on 125 consortia in the United States, including their program budgets, forms of governance, membership, and web pages. It is published by the Association for Consortium Leadership, the national organization of consortia whose mission includes the fostering of cooperation in higher education.

Dissertations

Belovarac, A. D. "Faculty and Administrative Roles in the Development of the Erie Consortium of Colleges." Unpublished doctoral dissertation, State University of New York at Buffalo, 1984.

In this case study, the author reports that the administration's attitudes and influences rather than the faculty's were the primary barriers to organizational success. Specifically, the lack of trust and the competitive attitudes of the participating institutional administrators ultimately led to undefined goals and the resulting lack of direction for the consortium.

Briggs, W. G. "The Marketing Role of the Bay Area Community College Television Consortium for Member Colleges (San Francisco)." Unpublished doctoral dissertation, University of San Francisco, 1983.

A number of studies have been conducted concerning the formation of consortia for the purpose of telecourse development and delivery. In this study, the author focuses on the success of the Bay Area Community College Television Consortium in the context of the marketing function. The author concludes that optimal benefits to the consortium may be attained through the formalizing of its goals and objectives, involving the campus presidents, broadening the faculty's understanding of televised instruction, and the expansion of market toward meeting a goal of self-sufficiency.

Courson, F. L. "A Benefits Assessment of Cross-Registration Programs in Six Multi-Purpose/Academic Consortia." Unpublished doctoral dissertation, The University of Alabama, 1982.

Cross-registration is one of the most common programs of consortia. This author describes and assesses the benefits of cross-registration programs in six multipurpose academic consortia. Also included are formulas for determining an estimate of derived dollar value from such programs.

Godbey, G. C. "Incentive Systems and Faculty Participation in Postsecondary Consortia." Unpublished doctoral dissertation, University of Pennsylvania, 1986.

In this study of two consortia, differences in administrative support, institutional prestige, faculty incentives, and faculty participation are considered. The more active consortium had more faculty who had a positive perception of administrative support and a recognition of more incentives to cooperate; the result was greater faculty participation. Institutional prestige, in this case study, was identified as an impediment toward consortial development.

Hanson, C. N. "The Associated Colleges of Central Kansas, 1966–1985: A Case Study." Unpublished doctoral dissertation, University of Kansas, 1986.

In addition to providing a twenty-year history of the Associated Colleges of Central Kansas, this dissertation also discusses the many accomplishments and factors that have contributed to its success. Factors identified include the individual growth of member institutions; active participation and support from administrators, faculty, and staff; and a diversity of activities.

Olk, P. M. "The Formation Process of Research and Development Consortia." Unpublished doctoral dissertation, University of Pennsylvania, 1991.

Data from fifty research and development consortia in the United States contributed to the author's five-stage model for the formation of interorganizational relations. The study also addresses the interaction between environmental constraints and strategic choices.

O'Malley, T. L. "The Effects of Consortium Fund-Raising in Independent Higher Education." Unpublished doctoral dissertation, University of Oregon, 1991.

Competition from state-supported higher education institutions has led independent colleges and universities to rely on joint fundraising efforts. This study presents factors that influenced the fundraising success of the Oregon Independent College Foundation and its eight member institutions: communication between the foundation's members and donors, prospect identification, and donor recognition.

INDEX

Back Issue/Subscription Order Form

Copy or detach and send to:
Jossey-Bass Inc., Publishers, 350 Sansome Street, San Francisco CA 94104-1342

Call or fax toll free!
Phone 888-378-2537 6AM-5PM PST; Fax 800-605-2665

Back issues: Please send me the following issues at $23 each.
(Important: please include series initials and issue number, such as HE90.)

1. HE _____

_____

_____

$ _____ Total for single issues

$ _____ Shipping charges (for single issues *only;* subscriptions are exempt
from shipping charges): Up to $30, add $5^{50} • $30^{01}–$50, add $6^{50}
$50^{01}–$75, add $7^{50} • $75^{01}–$100, add $9 • $100^{01}–$150, add $10
Over $150, call for shipping charge.

Subscriptions   Please ❏ start   ❏ renew my subscription to *New Directions
for Higher Education* for the year 19___ at the following rate:

    ❏ Individual $56   ❏ Institutional $99
NOTE: Subscriptions are quarterly, and are for the calendar year only.
Subscriptions begin with the spring issue of the year indicated above.
For shipping outside the U.S., please add $25.

$ _____ Total single issues and subscriptions (CA, IN, NJ, NY, and DC
residents, add sales tax for single issues. NY and DC residents must
include shipping charges when calculating sales tax. NY and Canadian
residents only, add sales tax for subscriptions.)

❏ Payment enclosed (U.S. check or money order only)
❏ VISA, MC, AmEx, Discover Card #_____ Exp. date_____

Signature _____ Day phone _____
❏ Bill me (U.S. institutional orders only. Purchase order required.)
Purchase order #_____

Name _____
Address _____

_____

Phone_____ E-mail _____

For more information about Jossey-Bass Publishers, visit our Web site at:
www.josseybass.com   **PRIORITY CODE = ND1**